The Dynamics of Social Norms

The Dynamics of Social Norms

H. PEYTON YOUNG

OXFORD
UNIVERSITY PRESS

OXFORD
UNIVERSITY PRESS

Great Clarendon Street, Oxford, OX2 6DP,
United Kingdom

Oxford University Press is a department of the University of Oxford.
It furthers the University's objective of excellence in research, scholarship,
and education by publishing worldwide. Oxford is a registered trade mark of
Oxford University Press in the UK and in certain other countries.

Published in the United States of America by Oxford University Press
546 Fifth Avenue, New York, NY 10036, United States of America

British Library Cataloguing in Publication Data

Data available

Library of Congress Control Number: 2026946821

ISBN 9780198959052

DOI: 10.1093/oso/9780198959052.001.0001

Printed and bound by
CPI Group (UK) Ltd., Croydon, CR0 4YY

The manufacturer's authorized representative in the EU for product safety is
Oxford University Press España S.A. of Parque Empresarial San Fernando de Henares,
Avenida de Castilla, 2 – 28830 Madrid (www.oup.es/en or product.safety@oup.com).
OUP España S.A. also acts as importer into Spain of products made by the manufacturer.

FSC www.fsc.org
MIX
Paper | Supporting responsible forestry
FSC® C013604

For my grandchildren

Jack, Gabriel, Chase, and Miles

Preface

This book presents a framework for studying the dynamics of social norms: how they arise, why they persist, and what causes them to change. Social norms have been extensively studied by sociologists, anthropologists, political scientists, and philosophers, but it is only recently that norms have become a focus of research by economists. This actually amounts to a revival of interest because the founders of the discipline were well aware that norms shape economic decisions. They affect the choice of career, levels of compensation, educational attainment, and the structure of economic contracts. They also enter into people's life choices: whether to get married or divorced, how many children to have, and when to retire. In short, norms have a profound impact on economic and social welfare.

I shall argue that normative influences can be incorporated into economics without giving up the idea that individuals act purposively and for the most part rationally. When people are embedded in social groups, rationality must include how you expect others to react to what you do. There is a fundamental feedback loop between own and others' behavior. This is, of course, the subject of game theory. The type of game theory I shall employ is a distinctive branch known as evolutionary game theory, which is concerned with both equilibrium and out-of-equilibrium behavior in populations of interacting players. Unlike conventional equilibrium analysis, this framework provides an explanation of how equilibria arise dynamically from arbitrary initial conditions, and how transitions between equilibria occur. Players are assumed to respond more or less rationally to their perceived environment, but they are not all-knowing or perfectly rational. They are adaptive. Over time their interactions produce complex dynamics that lead to equilibria at the population level; moreover, some of these equilibria are more likely to emerge than others independently of the initial conditions.

I originally became interested in the evolutionary point of view when teaching game theory to graduate students. One of the most beautiful results in the game theory canon is the explanation of how rational players come to play the Nash bargaining solution. Players alternate making offers and counteroffers, and after each period there is a small chance that the bargaining will break down. Each knows the other's utility function, each knows that the other knows it, and so forth. Each expects the other to behave rationally, each knows that the other expects rational behavior, and so on. The upshot is that they play something very close to the Nash bargaining solution in the very first period.

But is this how people bargain in practice? I spent my boyhood on a farm in Ohio that raises corn and soybeans. In that part of the country the customary way of compensating the tenant farmer is to divide the output in equal shares: half for the tenant, half for the landlord. It is known as "farming on the halves." It is a contractual norm that anchors the expectations of both sides. However, it doesn't seem to fit the classical game theory model very well because the latter predicts that the outcomes will be tailored to the bargainers' utilities, risk preferences, and outside options. In short, the outcomes will be heterogeneous. But this is not what we see in practice: the outcomes tend to be highly concentrated on particular focal shares that play the role of social norms. A similar phenomenon arises in many other types of compensation arrangements, such as real estate agents' commissions, lawyers' fees, and bonus payments for financial managers (see Chapter 6).

The question is how such norms arise, why they are followed, and how much they depart from neoclassical predictions. This book provides a simple but general framework for addressing these issues. A central feature of the framework is a positive feedback loop linking individual and group behavior: the more people in one's reference group who act in a particular way, the greater the inclination of others to follow suit. The precise mechanisms underlying this process are, however, highly varied and context dependent. I do not subscribe to the view that deviations from a norm must invariably be enforced by targeted, costly "punishment." Norm violations have negative consequences, but they do not necessarily entail explicit and deliberate punishment by others. In some cases, there is an *inherent* cost to miscoordination that requires no punishment by third parties. In other cases, there is a *reputational* cost to norm violation that invites social disapproval or a negative assessment of one's personal qualities, but that requires little or no effort on the part of others. In still other cases, norm-following behavior may be instilled from one generation to another through a process of *cultural transmission*. And in some situations, norm-following is just an expedient way of making decisions that are difficult to rationalize from fundamentals. These and other mechanisms are not mutually exclusive; in fact, they often operate in tandem to sustain a given normative behavior.

The resulting dynamics display distinctive characteristics. First, norms tend to be highly persistent, and are relatively impervious to changes in exogenous conditions that in principle should change individual incentives and behavior.

Second, norms mask heterogeneity in individual preferences because conforming to group behavior confers benefits that outweigh the gains from idiosyncratic choices. The result is *excess uniformity* in behavior as compared to standard neoclassical predictions. Third, when norm shifts occur, they often do so quite suddenly as a tipping point is reached where one norm gives way to another. These three effects—persistence, excess uniformity, and tipping—can be tested empirically to ascertain whether norms are at work in specific settings.

In subsequent chapters I explore these implications in a variety of concrete cases, including norms of attire, tipping, dueling, circumcision, principal–agent contracts, consumer choice, and many others. I shall touch briefly (in Chapter 3) on the application of the framework to norms of cooperation, but a full examination of this topic would require a separate treatment.[1] Rather, the focus of the present work is to study norm formation and norm shifts across a wide array of examples where the *coordination* of expectations and behaviors is the key driving force.

As the examples in subsequent chapters will demonstrate, norm shifts are triggered by an accumulation of changes in behavior that eventually reach a critical threshold or "tipping point," after which the new norm rapidly displaces the old due to positive feedback effects. In some cases, the process is set in motion by the actions of specific individuals. In other cases, the changes are uncoordinated and more or less spontaneous. And sometimes a norm shift is instigated by a deliberate and coordinated intervention that seeks to alter the perceived payoffs from following a given norm, or that alters its meaning and significance. The resulting dynamics depend on the network through which people interact, as well as on the extent to which individual behaviors are somewhat unpredictable due to mistakes, misperceptions, payoff shocks, and other random influences.

The book is intended to be a primer and does not presuppose extensive mathematical background, although a taste for logical argument and some familiarity with basic concepts from game theory would help. The theoretical framework is discussed at a nontechnical level and is motivated by a series of examples; technical details and proofs can be found in my books *Individual Strategy and Social Structure* (1998) and *Spontaneous Order* (2024). Empirical

[1] For book-length treatments of cooperative norms see among others Axelrod 1984, Ostrom 1990, Bicchieri et al. 1996; Skyrms 1996, 2004; Hechter and Opp 2001; Henrich et al. 2004, Boyd and Richerson 2006; Bicchieri 2006; Henrich and Henrich 2007, Bowles and Gintis 2011; Ensminger and Henrich, eds., 2014.

cases are introduced at an informal, descriptive level in order to illustrate common themes, and to raise awareness of the extent to which we are embedded in a complex web of norms that shape our everyday behaviors, often without being fully conscious of them. In some cases, notably those treated in Chapters 6 and 8, the data allow us to model normative forces in some detail; in other cases the narratives are suggestive but more data would be needed to measure the extent to which norms are operating. My hope is that these accounts will spur others to take up the challenge of incorporating norms more fully into economic analysis, and to gather the data needed to measure their influence in concrete cases.

Acknowledgments

This book draws on the contributions of many others. The key concept of stochastic stability discussed in Chapter 3 was formulated with my long-time collaborator Dean Foster. Chapter 4 on experiments testing stochastic stability was co-authored with Heinrich Nax. Chapter 5 on tipping points and transition times is based on joint work with Itai Arieli, Yakov Babichenko, Gabriel Kreindler, and Ron Peretz. Chapter 6 on norms of compensation is based in part on joint work with Mary Burke on contractual norms in agriculture. Chapter 7 on costly norms was co-authored with Sam Jindani. Chapter 8 on female genital circumcision in Somalia is based on joint work with Selim Gulesci, Sam Jindani, Eliana La Ferrara, David Smerdon, and Munshi Suleiman.

More generally, the analytical framework builds on an extensive literature on social interactions and evolutionary game theory developed by George Akerlof, Robert Akerlof, Ken Binmore, Lawrence Blume, William Brock, Steven Durlauf, Michihiro Kandori, George Mailath, Rafael Rob, Larry Samuelson, Brian Skyrms, Fernando Vega-Redondo, and Jorgen Weibull. The overall approach, which combines formal analysis with narrative accounts, was inspired by the work of Thomas Schelling, who pioneered the application of social interaction models to the study of sociological and economic phenomena.

The manuscript has greatly benefited from the comments and criticisms of colleagues and students. I particularly wish to thank Sam Bowles, Damon Centola, Sam Jindani, Rachel Kranton, Heinrich Nax, Tom Norman, Bary Pradelski, Ariel Rubenstein, Brian Skyrms, Ludvig Sinander, Bassel Tarbush, and David Vines for giving it a close reading and suggesting improvements in the presentation. I take full responsibility for any remaining errors.

Contents

1

What Are Social Norms?

Norm. A pattern of behavior that is usual or expected.
Oxford English Dictionary

1.1 The web of norms

Social norms govern our interactions with others. They are the unwritten rules, informal understandings, and implicit agreements that define what we expect of others and what they expect of us. Norms establish obligations to family members, property rights, contractual relationships, conceptions of right and wrong, notions of fairness, the meanings of words, obedience to the law. They are the building blocks of social order.

Despite their prevalence, however, social norms are so embedded in our everyday ways of thinking and doing things that we often follow them unconsciously, routinely, reflexively, and with little deliberation. They are conditioned on who we are, where we are, and whom we interact with. We learn appropriate normative behaviors in much the same way that we learn a language; indeed, many norms function as a language that communicates identity, values, personal attributes, and beliefs. Norm violations raise doubts about who we are and what values we hold. Moreover, those who violate particular norms may not be attentive to norms in general and therefore cannot be relied upon. Norm-following is itself a norm.

Although norms are a prominent feature of the societies customarily studied by anthropologists, we sometimes imagine that in the large-scale, market-oriented societies that many of us inhabit, norms have largely faded away. The reality is quite different: we are embedded in a complex web of social norms that guide our behavior and affect our decisions, sometimes very consequential decisions, but we often fail to see how much we are in their power. Social norms enter into our choice of profession and the level of education we pursue. They affect levels of pay in different professions. They are a feature of economic

This chapter is based in part on H. P. Young 2015.

The Dynamics of Social Norms. H. Peyton Young, Oxford University Press.
 DOI: 10.1093/oso/9780198959052.003.0001

incentive contracts. They influence the age at which we get married, whether to have children out of wedlock, whether to get divorced, and when to retire. They are at work in such seemingly minor matters as what to wear to the office or to a dinner party, how much to tip the waiter, whether to hug someone or simply shake hands.

Norms also operate at the level of organizations and institutions: who gets access to higher education, who has the right to vote, who can get married, and who can own property. These and numerous other instances of "rights" are decided by institutions and polities rather than by individuals. There are powerful spillover effects between the institutions making such choices that are similar to the spillover effects between individual choices, and that lead in much the same way to the establishment of institutional norms through positive feedback effects (see Chapter 9).

In the following chapters I shall focus on concrete examples of this sort, whose meaning is determined by context, and whose evolution can be documented in some detail. Although some of these examples may seem rather specialized, in some cases even trivial, their violation can have significant reputational and material consequences. Such familiar, everyday examples can help guide our thinking about how social norms evolve and what mechanisms sustain them.

1.2 Norms as communication devices

Consider the current custom of US politicians wearing flag lapel pins. There was a time when lapel pins of any kind were rarely worn, and if they were, they often represented particular affiliations of the wearer, such as membership in associations, like the American Legion or the Elks. Beginning in the early 1970s, however, Republican candidates and office-holders began to wear flag lapel pins as a symbol of patriotic solidarity against Vietnam War protesters.[1] The trend was strengthened after the events of 9/11, President George W. Bush instructed his aides to wear flag lapel pins. Nowadays it is considered virtually mandatory by candidates for federal office, whether Republican or Democrat. Failure to conform may be construed as a negative signal of one's patriotism, and may well have consequences at the ballot box.

[1] The practice is sometimes attributed to Robert Redford, who displayed a flag lapel pin in the movie *The Candidate*. Soon thereafter Richard Nixon instructed his aides to wear them, and the custom continued to spread until it became established as a norm among US politicians (Ambrose 1989).

This example illustrates the point that once an ordinary and seemingly trivial act is adopted by enough people in a particular group, it can become invested with meaning. Not performing the act is interpreted—perhaps quite erroneously—as an indication of who you are and what values you hold. Norms that are imbued with such symbolic content can be very difficult to dislodge, and violating them can have serious adverse consequences. For example, in October 2007 presidential candidate Barack Obama was asked by a member of the press why he wasn't wearing a flag lapel pin. He responded:

> *I decided I won't wear that pin on my chest. Instead I'm going to try to tell the American people what I believe will make this country great and hopefully that will be a testimony to my patriotism . . . My attitude is that I'm less concerned about what you're wearing on your lapel than what's in your heart.*

His response prompted a public furore, and before long he was sporting a flag lapel pin at all of his public appearances.[2]

Another example of a norm with symbolic content is dueling.[3] Although it is now virtually extinct, dueling was common in Europe and the United States until well into the nineteenth century. No fewer than four British prime ministers participated in duels: William Petty, William Pitt the Younger, George Canning, and Arthur Wellesley (Duke of Wellington). Two of them—Pitt and Wellesley—dueled while holding public office. Abraham Lincoln narrowly avoided a duel when his seconds managed to reconcile the parties at the last moment. Famously, Aaron Burr challenged Alexander Hamilton to a duel after an attack on his character that he attributed to Hamilton. Although Hamilton was morally opposed to dueling and felt it would be irresponsible toward his family to engage in one, he felt that he had to go ahead anyway. To ignore the challenge would almost certainly damage his public standing and political career. In the end he was killed.

I shall revisit the case of dueling in more detail in Chapter 7, but the main features can be summarized here. First, the act itself was dangerous: the chances of being killed or wounded were substantial. Second, the norm was held in place by the prospect of losing status amongst one's peers. Dueling was particularly common among those in the public eye, notably politicians and journalists. Third, the norm was governed by a complex web of ancillary norms: the role of seconds, the choice of weapons, and the number of paces separating the duelists. Fourth, the practice persisted for centuries in spite of

[2] Newton-Small 2008.
[3] This account is based on Banks 2008, 2012, Chernow 2004 and Hopton 2007.

being illegal in most jurisdictions. In France, for example, it was outlawed at least nine times over the course of the eighteenth and nineteenth centuries, to no avail. Yet by the twentieth century the practice had almost entirely disappeared, a spontaneous change that has been attributed to changing social attitudes toward masculine codes of honor more generally.[4]

Consider another, more contemporary, example. Female genital cutting is still widely practiced in sub-Saharan Africa, the Middle East and parts of southeast Asia, and affects several hundred million women worldwide.[5] Cutting takes several different forms, some of which are highly invasive, entail serious medical risks, and can lead to life-long pain and suffering. Nevertheless, in many communities being cut confers important social benefits: it is a marker of "purification" and serves as admission to the social network of adult women. It may also enhance a girl's future marriage prospects. Girls who are not cut are routinely subjected to mocking, shunning, and accusations of impurity by other girls. For example, an ethnographic study of female genital cutting in Senegal and the Gambia found that "those who are not circumcised are contemptuously insulted by being labeled *solima*, meaning not only uncircumcised, but also rude, ignorant, immature, uncivilized, and unclean; women who are *solima* are told they know nothing and are harassed and excluded by women for not knowing how to behave properly."[6] Thus social pressure creates a strong incentive to follow the prevailing norm even though it can cause significant personal harm. Although in recent years there has been a transition away from the most harmful forms of FGC, it is still widely practiced, and the transition dynamics appear to be substituting one version of the norm by another less drastic (but still harmful) variant, as we shall see in Chapter 8.

Another example of a contemporary norm that affects women in developing countries is the use of contraception. Although the means of contraception are widely available and quite inexpensive, the uptake in some communities has been very slow because it is viewed as a violation of norms about the appropriate role of women as child-bearers. A woman who wants to limit the number of children by contraception, say to gain more education or to enter the workforce, may be deterred by the social opprobrium heaped on her by other members of her social group. Demographic studies find that these norms operate more strongly in some communities than others. It follows

[4] Nye 1993.
[5] See among others Mackie 1996, Shell-Duncan 2001, 2011, Gele, Bo, and Sundby 2013, Gulesci et al. 2025.
[6] Shell-Duncan et al. 2011, pp. 7–8.

that a woman's willingness to use contraception within a given community is not merely determined by economic variables, such as access to education or employment opportunities; it is also strongly influenced by the social attitudes of other members in the community and by the prevalence of the practice among her peers.[7] The result is that communities with similar economic and demographic characteristics sometimes exhibit very different rates of uptake. This is a general feature of social norms called *local conformity/global diversity* that we shall observe in many other settings.

The preceding four examples—lapel pins, dueling, FGC, and contraception—are very different, yet in each case they are imbued with specific meanings. Norm violation is taken to be a negative indicator of the violator's values, character, or identity. In some situations the indicator may be completely spurious—whether or not one wears a flag lapel pin may have nothing to do with the wearer's actual patriotism. Nevertheless, deviation from the norm can have deleterious consequences for the norm violator's reputation. In other situations, such as dueling, the act may provide noisy information about an underlying trait (such as bravery). In both cases the feedback effects between individual and group behavior are similar: the more common it is to follow a norm, the more negative the reputational consequences from violating it.[8]

1.3 The evolution of norms

What then is a social norm? It is an equilibrium that coordinates expectations and behaviors within a social group. People adhere to their prescribed role in the equilibrium, they expect others to adhere to their roles, and it is in their interest to adhere to these roles given the negative consequences of deviating. But how do group-level behaviors and expectations come into equilibrium starting from out-of-equilibrium conditions? Which equilibria are most likely to emerge when many potential equilibria exist? Although much of economics is concerned with the properties of equilibria, it is usually silent

[7] See among others Kohler 1997, 2000, Kohler, Berman, and Watkins 2001, Munshi and Myaux 2006.

[8] This idea can be formalized in a signaling model, whereby an individual's behavior leads to an inference about an underlying but unobservable characteristic (Bernheim 1994). Such models typically have multiple equilibria, which depend on the distribution of the characteristic in the population, as well as on individual preferences for being seen to have that characteristic. In what follows I shall adopt a general model of social interactions in which deviations from a norm have payoff consequences that can arise for a variety of reasons, including negative reputational effects, but that does not pre-suppose that people make statistical inferences about others' personal characteristics.

on how such equilibria come about. The emergence of equilibrium is one of the central questions addressed in this book, using social norms as the object of study.

The question of what norms are, and how they evolve, has a long history. One of the earliest discussions of the matter is due to David Hume in his *Treatise on Human Nature* (1739):

> I observe, that it will be for my interest to leave another in the possession of his goods, *provided* he will act in the same manner with regard to me. He is sensible of a like interest in the regulation of his conduct. When this common sense of interest is mutually express'd, and is known to both, it produces a suitable resolution and behavior. And this may properly enough be call'd a convention or agreement betwixt us, tho' without the interposition of a promise; since the actions of each of us have a reference to those of the other, and are perform'd upon the supposition, that something is to be perform'd on the other part. Two men, who pull the oars of a boat, do it by an agreement or convention, tho' they have never given promises to each other. Nor is the rule concerning the stability of possession the less deriv'd from human conventions, that it arises gradually, and acquires force by a slow progression, and by our repeated experience of the inconveniences of transgressing it. On the contrary, this experience assures us still more, that the sense of interest has become common to all our fellows, and gives us a confidence of the future regularity of their conduct . . . In like manner are languages gradually establish'd by human conventions without any promise. In like manner do gold and silver become the common measures of exchange.[9]

In this remarkable passage Hume identifies four key factors in the evolution of social norms (or in his terminology, conventions):[10] i) they are equilibria of particular forms of interaction; ii) they evolve through a process of learning from experience; iii) they acquire force through repetition; iv) they underpin many forms of social and economic order, including language, money, and property rights. In a later passage Hume even asserts that concepts of morality are socially constructed in much the same fashion, a view that got him into considerable difficulty with the religious authorities of the day. (He was denied a chair in philosophy at the University of Glasgow due to his supposed atheism.)

[9] Hume 1739.

[10] By "convention" Hume means a tacit agreement. Hume's remarkable claim is that the most fundamental aspects of social order (including morality) are ultimately just conventions.

In subsequent chapters I shall show how these questions can be addressed more generally using the tools of evolutionary game theory. In particular, the theory shows how norms can emerge spontaneously from the decentralized interactions of many individuals. Norm shifts may be triggered by the actions of a few individuals, after which they coalesce on their own through a process of social diffusion, or they may simply bubble up from below. In either case, the theory predicts that some norms are more likely to emerge than others because they are inherently more stable against random fluctuations. The theory also shows that norm dynamics possess certain signature features that can be used to assess empirically whether norms are likely to be present in a given setting.[11]

1.4 Signature features of norm dynamics

Persistence. Norms tend to persist for long periods, and they respond very sluggishly to changes in external conditions that alter the benefits and costs of adhering to the norm. For example, persistence is a striking feature of certain contractual norms, such as customary shares for landowners and tenants in agricultural contracts, percentages charged by tort lawyers in malpractice and product liability cases, performance fees charged by fund managers, commissions for real estate agents, and so forth (see Chapter 6). Once established by precedent, such shares can persist for many years in spite of changing economic conditions. Norms of cooperation and mutual trust, or the lack thereof, can persist for centuries once they are established in a given society, as can norms that support persistent inequalities between social classes.[12] This feature can provide a basis for testing the plausibility that a given behavior is a norm: it remains rigidly in place in spite of changing incentives that would be expected to alter individual behavior were group feedback effects not present.

Sudden shifts. A second signature feature of norm dynamics is that, when change does occur, the transition tends to be abrupt rather than incremental. The reason is that once a sufficient number of people in a given social group have changed their behavior, positive feedback reinforces the new way of doing things and the transition tends to be completed rapidly. Schelling referred to this phenomenon as "tipping," a term that was coined in the 1950s to describe

[11] This framework builds on dynamic models of equilibrium selection due to Foster and Young 1990, Young 1993a, Kandori et al. 1993, Ellison 1993, and Blume 1993, 1997. For textbook treatments of evolutionary game theory see Vega-Redondo 1996, Samuelson 1997, Weibull 1997, Hofbauer and Sigmund 1998, Young 1998a, and Sandholm 2010.

[12] Banfield 1958, Putnam 1993, Tabellini 2008, Guiso et al. 2009, Acemoglu and Robinson 2012, Belloc and Bowles 2013, Hwang et al. 2024.

sudden changes in the racial composition of city neighborhoods.[13] Sometimes it suffices for just a few people to initiate the change, which then spreads by contagion through a much larger group. As will be shown in Chapter 5, the dynamics of norm transition are complex, and depend on the network through which people interact, as well as on the extent to which they deviate from best-response behavior due to idiosyncratic influences and random shocks.

In combination, these two features of norm dynamics—persistence and tipping—create a characteristic *signature* in the historical evolution of norms: there are long periods of little or no change that are occasionally interrupted by bursts of activity in which an old norm is rapidly displaced by a new one. I call this the *punctuated equilibrium effect*.[14] For example, the footbinding of women was a norm in China for over a thousand years; yet the practice was largely abandoned within just two generations in the early twentieth century. In our own times, attitudes toward same-sex marriage have undergone a radical shift in just a few decades.

Excess uniformity (compression). Norms cause people within a social group to behave similarly even though, in the absence of social interactions, they would exhibit diverse behaviors due to differences in preferences and personal circumstances. In other words, norms suppress heterogeneity and lead to excess uniformity in behavior. I call this the *compression effect*.

To illustrate, consider historic norms of dueling, which was an accepted way of settling scores among aristocrats, politicians, and military officers until well into the nineteenth century. It is reasonable to suppose that duelists varied considerably in their degree of risk aversion, marksmanship, the hardship imposed on their families if they were wounded or killed, and so forth. Nevertheless, the terms of a duel were clearly established by convention, not bargained over to reflect the idiosyncratic preferences of the duelists. Even small departures from established practice, such as dueling at 15 paces instead of 10, would be considered a breach of protocol, and have negative repercussions for the duelists' reputations. This phenomenon—excessively uniform behavior in spite of idiosyncratic differences—is a characteristic feature of norms.

To take another example, if landowners and tenants did not gravitate toward normative share contracts in a given locality, such as half-half, or one-third:two-thirds, one would expect to see considerable diversity in contract terms, depending on underlying fundamentals such as the quality of land and

[13] Schelling 1978.
[14] Young 1998a. In biology this term has a more specific interpretation; here I use it to describe the characteristic look of a dynamical path.

labor inputs, risk aversion, and the value of the parties' outside options. A similar tendency toward uniformity can be observed in many other settings that ought in theory to be competitively negotiated, including bonus fees for hedge fund managers, commissions for real estate agents, and fees for tort lawyers (see Chapter 6).[15]

Local conformity/global diversity. Although norms tend to promote conformity within a given social group, they may lead to substantial differences in behavior across groups that have little interaction with one another but are otherwise similar. This phenomenon arises from the fact that a given type of social interaction often admits multiple coordination equilibria; the one that actually emerges is due to chance events and path dependencies that lead (at least in the intermediate run) to different outcomes across groups. This effect is known as *local conformity/global diversity.* For example, in the latter part of the nineteenth century, the norms surrounding dueling, including the choice of weapons and the terms of engagement, were substantially different in France and in Britain (for details see Chapter 7). Both served a similar social role as male codes of honor, and they could co-exist because the relevant social groups were sufficiently disjoint. Similarly, norms of contraception and child-bearing differ substantially between social groups that are otherwise similar, as has been documented by field studies of village-level behaviors in Africa and India.[16]

1.5 Mechanisms underpinning social norms

The empirical phenomena discussed above all flow from a central feature of social norm dynamics, namely, they exhibit increasing returns. The more people who exhibit a particular behavior in a given social group, the more people come to expect that this behavior will be followed by others in that group, and the more desirable it becomes to behave in that way too. In other words, norms solve coordination problems. In some cases, the benefits arise from physical coordination, such as what side of the road to drive on, whether to shake hands, hug, or touch noses, or what time to go to lunch. In other cases, norms coordinate the meaning and interpretation that people place on different forms of behavior, as well as on the appropriate responses to norm violation. Which of these mechanisms is operative depends very much on context; in fact, several

[15] For econometric tests of the compression effect see Graham 2008.
[16] Kohler, Berman, and Watkins 2001, Munshi and Myaux 2006.

different mechanisms may be operating in tandem. In what follows I consider several of these mechanisms in more detail.

Punishment, censure, and reputation. Norm violations may have negative social consequences that act as a powerful incentive to adhere to a prevailing norm. These social mechanisms take a variety of forms. In some cases, violations are met with targeted and severe forms of punishment, such as ostracism, shunning, or violence. Deviants may be driven out of the community, subjected to physical assault, or even killed. In some traditional religious communities, for example, those who marry outside the faith may be permanently banished. In Mafia culture, breaking the code of silence by cooperating with or giving information to authorities can be punishable by death. Such severe forms of punishment typically require coordinated action by other members of the community, and may even call for penalties for those who do not participate in the enforcement activity. In fact, severe forms of punishment may themselves be regulated by norms that determine what measures are appropriate in particular cases.[17]

More commonly, norm violations trigger expressions of disapproval, gossip, and ridicule that require little or no coordinated effort, but have a strong negative impact on the reputation and social standing of the deviant. Alexander Hamilton worried that refusing Burr's challenge to a duel would lead to such widespread negative comment within his social circle that he would rather risk his life than suffer the ensuing damage to his reputation and social standing (see Chapter 7). The Somalian girl who declines to be circumcised can expect to be mocked, ridiculed, and labeled as "unclean" by other females in the community, which constitutes (for many) enough of a deterrent to submit to the procedure in spite of its serious health risks (see Chapter 8). Obama's refusal to wear a flag lapel pin triggered such negative reaction in the press that he quickly reversed course for fear that it would severely damage his political prospects.

A more subtle mechanism holding norms in place is that deviations lead to negative opinions about a person's character, values, or identity, even though people may not express them openly. When roller bags were first introduced, for example, most men refused to use them because of their feminine associations (they were typically used by airline stewardesses), but there was no need for anyone to mention the implications explicitly (see Chapter 2). The person who wears inappropriate attire to a dinner party, or uses bad table manners, will probably not be openly rebuked, but they may be seen as unreliable and

[17] Mathew and Boyd 2014, Mathew 2017.

insensitive to social norms in general. Even if Obama's refusal to wear a lapel pin had not attracted public criticism, it might have hurt his political prospects. People would think him unpatriotic and be less inclined to vote for him, not as a form of retribution, but simply because they now have a less favorable opinion of him. Under this "inferential" mechanism, deviations from customary and expected behavior are interpreted by others in a negative way without any explicit punishment or censure being applied. Norm violations lead to pejorative inferences about a person's character, and people care about what others think of them.[18]

Heuristic decision-making. Norms of behavior can result from heuristic aids to decision-making that are followed when there is no clear basis for making an optimal decision. A classic example is the prominence of 50:50 division when two people are faced with the problem of how to divide a pie. In Chapter 6 I shall examine how such norms operate in the marketplace, that is, how they structure the terms of contracts and commissions between buyers and sellers, principals and clients, or tenants and landlords.[19] It is sometimes overlooked, however, that people routinely use *socially constructed* reference points for making decisions.[20] These typically take the form of targets, benchmarks, or thresholds, such as how much to save for retirement, when to take retirement, when to get married, or how many children to have. Such benchmarks lead to norms of behavior that derive their salience from the fact that they are widely used by others. They present a convenient way of making (and justifying) decisions that most people would find difficult to solve in a fully rational manner, that is, by considering all the relevant costs and benefits. Imitating others also avoids the uncertainties and potential risks associated with alternative, less established ways of behaving. Thus, as in the previous cases, there is a powerful feedback loop between the behaviors of the group and the actions of the individual; in this sense they are socially constructed.

Consider, for example, the choice of retirement age. In the United States, and indeed in many other countries, the standard retirement age used to be 65. This can be traced to the pension system devised by Bismarck in the 1880s.[21]

[18] Krupke and Weber 2013 show that subjects take into account how they think others will evaluate the "appropriateness" of their actions (and sacrifice money payments accordingly), even though there is no opportunity for the others to openly express their disapproval.

[19] In the literature these are sometimes referred to as "descriptive" norms: deviations are costly due to coordination failure but they do not trigger social disapproval.

[20] See among others Kahneman et al. 1982 and Gigerenzer et al. 1999.

[21] In fact, the original age in the German system was 70; later Bismarck reduced it to 65 as a way of getting rid of several senior military generals (Cohen 1957, Myers 1973). The diffusion of policies from one jurisdiction to another via imitation is a well-documented feature of many policy innovations, as will be discussed in Chapter 9.

Subsequently many countries copied various features of the German system in their own retirement arrangements, and 65 became a convenient reference point (norm) for those designing the retirement systems, and also for the individuals within these systems once 65 became embedded in the public consciousness. Moreover, the normative aspect continued even when the incentives supporting it had been removed. For example, in the early 1960s the retirement system in the United States was changed so that the expected benefits remained essentially the same for anyone retiring between 62 and 65. Nevertheless many people did not take advantage of the change: the distribution of retirement ages continued to have a spike at 65 until well into the 1990s. Once 65 had become fixed in the public mind as the "normal" age to retire, it continued to serve as a heuristic for many years after it had ceased to have any particular economic benefit.[22] Furthermore it had a potential coordination benefit, namely, retiring when one's friends retire.

In short, norms can be held in place by a variety of mechanisms, including outright punishment, gossip and ridicule, a desire to coordinate, or just an expedient way of making decisions. The key to understanding norm dynamics is the existence of a positive feedback loop between social and individual behaviors, whatever its source.

1.6 Norm shifts

The norms that we see at a given place and time are the result of an evolutionary process that is shaped by a combination of random events, changing external circumstances, and individual choices. Once a norm is in place it will tend to persist for a long period precisely because it is an equilibrium at the level of the group.

How then do norm shifts occur? Sometimes norms change through the actions of influential individuals and trend-setters. This is particularly true of changes in fashion (see Chapter 2). Frequently, however, norm shifts occur through a gradual, scattered, uncoordinated, alteration in people's behaviors without any top-down direction. Once enough of these changes accumulate, an old norm is displaced by a new one. For example, when I first joined a new research group at the US Treasury Department in 2012, almost all the men wore coat and tie to work. Over a period of several years, however, the

[22] Axtell and Epstein 1999, Burtless 2006. Similarly, one could argue that reliance on "top five" publications has become a norm of convenience among economics departments for making hiring and tenure decisions.

dress code within the research group gradually eroded. First one or two people (usually the younger ones) would show up with a jacket but no tie. By the next year this practice had spread to almost everyone. Then a few people started coming into work in slacks and no jacket. Within a year this had become the new norm. The change was no doubt facilitated by a broader trend toward more casual business attire in society at large; nevertheless, the norm shift within the research group followed its own internal dynamic whereby changes within the group led others to follow suit. Furthermore, this transition did not occur in some other parts of the Treasury Department, where greater formality remained the norm.

Many other norm shifts occur in a similar fashion: they bubble up from below rather than are led from above. To take another example, not so long ago it was rare for an American audience to give performers a standing ovation. They were reserved only for the most outstanding of performances. Then a gradual change occurred in which more and more people spontaneously decided to express their approval by standing up, which led others to stand up too (lest they be thought unenthusiastic). Nowadays the standing ovation has become customary, almost obligatory: not to stand would be interpreted by the performers as an expression of disappointment. It is a form of grade inflation. It is also reinforced because those who choose to stand block the view of those behind. Even if the latter were not particularly enthused by the performance, they want to see the performers take a bow. Thus the norm is enforced through a combination of symbolic and physical coordination.

1.7 Interventions

Norm shifts are sometimes instigated by deliberate and coordinated forms of intervention. This is particularly relevant when a norm is harmful to individuals, but is maintained by social pressure to conform. The theoretical framework developed in this book provides some guidance to the forms of intervention that may be effective in overturning such norms. However, the theory also highlights the complexity of this task and the fact that some "obvious" solutions may not work very well. In what follows I consider some of the potential instruments of intervention, as well as some of their limitations. The key point is that it is not enough to create new and better equilibria of the system, as in conventional theories of mechanism design. One must also consider the dynamics by which adjustment to these new equilibria may (or may not) take place.

Taxes and penalties. Perhaps the most obvious form of intervention is to tax or otherwise penalize deleterious forms of behavior that are entrenched as social norms. In the case of dueling, the practice was outlawed in many countries and on numerous occasions. It turned out, however, that the penalties were difficult to enforce and simply drove the practice "underground"; in fact, those responsible for carrying out the penalties were often sympathetic to the practice. In the current drive to eliminate female genital cutting (FGC), various interventions of this type have been tried, including making the practice illegal, and paying professional cutters not to cut. As in the case of dueling, these measures have proved to be difficult to enforce in practice, especially in countries where enforcement institutions are weak. Furthermore, bans and taxes may backfire: for example, imposing a luxury tax on super-yachts could actually increase their desirability for the super-rich.

Leadership. An alternative approach is to induce community leaders to take a stand against a harmful normative practice, or to set an example by publicly violating an established norm. Although this would seem to be an obvious and relatively low-cost strategy, the difficulty is that leaders are often very sensitive to public opinion and may therefore be reluctant to buck prevailing norms: witness Obama's short-lived attempt to undo the norm of wearing flag lapel pins. More generally, it is not sufficient that a given individual be connected to many other people. Of crucial importance is the overall network structure within which such potential influencers are embedded. As I show in Chapter 5, poorly connected individuals may be more likely than leaders to tip society into a new and more desirable norm. The new norm can spread by contagion from one poorly connected individual to another, in which case the would-be influencer ends up being a follower rather than a leader.

Local targeting. A crucial feature of norm dynamics is that they exhibit increasing returns. One way of leveraging this property is to target subgroups of individuals who interact closely with one another, rather than target a scattered subset of people who are only weakly connected. For example, if a society consists of loosely connected villages, it will be more effective to target many people in the same village rather than a few people in each village. The former strategy may achieve a critical mass and lead to norm change in some of the villages, whereas the latter may be insufficient to induce change in any of them. A version of this strategy was employed in the campaign against footbinding in China, which was seen as a way of enhancing the chances of a daughter's marriageability.[23] Opponents of the practice organized "natural

[23] Mackie 1996.

foot societies" at the local level, whose members made public pledges not to footbind their daughters, and not to permit their sons to marry footbound daughters. The concept was to break the norm within the group by creating shared expectations about others' intentions to change their behavior.

In both of the preceding types of intervention, the details of the social interaction structure matter in determining the most effective way of inducing a norm transition. In some cases, community leaders may be the best vehicle for inducing change (assuming they are willing to try), but this is not always so. In other cases, it may be more effective to target closely interacting subgroups ("villages"). In general, there is no simple and all-purpose approach to inducing norm shifts without taking into account the social network within which people are embedded.

Shifts in meaning. As I have repeatedly emphasized, social norms are often held in place because they have a specific meaning or significance, and violations lead to negative inferences about the violator's values, beliefs, or personal qualities. This suggests that a useful way to induce a norm shift is to change the perceived meaning of a given norm. For example, this approach was employed in the campaign to eradicate footbinding in China. The practice had traditionally been seen as a symbol of high family status, since the footbound woman was limited to sedentary forms of work. In the late nineteenth and early twentieth centuries opponents managed to re-cast the practice as outmoded, backward, and out-of-step at a time when China was looking to the West as a model of how to modernize.

More recently, opponents of FGC have enlisted the help of local Imams who have taken the position that less invasive and harmful forms of the practice (known as Sunna) are more consistent with Islam than the traditional and much more harmful form (known as Pharaonic). In this way the older norm is robbed of its significance as a signal of religious commitment. Note, however, that this strategy may not eliminate the practice entirely: it could lead to a new norm that is less harmful but still functions as an important rite of passage for young girls in the community, as will be discussed in Chapter 8. This example underscores the importance of modeling the full dynamics of norm adjustment, and not simply looking at the properties of different equilibria in isolation.

Information. Within any community there will inevitably be some diversity in behavior despite the presence of a norm. Most people follow the norm, but not everyone. This does not imply that a norm is not present; rather it means that there is heterogeneity in people's preferences and beliefs that leads some of them to deviate from normative behavior. Heterogeneity is a key feature of norm dynamics, and sometimes produces spontaneous shifts. These occur when unobserved payoff shocks and other perturbations accumulate to such an extent that a tipping point is reached and society transitions to the new norm without any intervention.

The provision of better information can accelerate the transition in some circumstances. In particular, people may be unaware of the cost of following a given norm. FGC is a case in point: surveys suggest that many families in Somalia were unaware of the potential health risks posed by the more extreme forms of FGC.[24] More generally, providing accurate information about the costs of a harmful norm may induce some people to give it up, thus initiating a cascade that leads to its collapse.

Another reason for providing information is to overcome pluralistic ignorance. Surveys show that people often overestimate the extent to which norms are actually followed in one's social group.[25] Providing information about how many people deviate from a normative practice may be enough to induce a dynamic in which the norm unravels on its own without any additional intervention. This point is intuitively obvious if surveys reveal that a large fraction of the population does not actually follow the norm. Less obvious is the fact that awareness of the existence of even a small proportion of norm violators may be enough to destabilize it. Suppose, for example, that a survey reveals that 5% of a given group are norm violators. Suppose also that 6% of the population would deviate if they thought the chances were at least 5% that their randomly drawn partner will deviate. (People's intentions do not need to be revealed in the survey, only the proportion of others that are currently deviating.) After a series of random encounters, the expected proportion of deviants will now be 6%. If this proportion is revealed in a new survey, it could be that 7% of the population will want to deviate. This leads, in expectation, to a new deviation rate of 7%, and so forth. In short, if there is sufficient heterogeneity in a population, then a norm shift can occur on its own, provided that people have sufficiently accurate information.[26]

In subsequent chapters I shall employ a combination of theory, experimental evidence, field data, and narrative accounts to help us understand how norm shifts occur in practice, and how norm shifts can sometimes be leveraged or speeded up through appropriate types of intervention.

[24] Gulesci et al. 2025

[25] Smerdon, Offerman, and Gneezy 2020, Burstyn, Gonzalez, and Yanagizawa-Drott 2020.

[26] Providing more information does not necessarily lead to norm unraveling; in fact, the opposite may occur and the norm may become further entrenched. For example, the original 5% of deviants might induce only 4% to deviate, which induces only 3% to deviate and so forth.

2

Norms and Identity

2.1 The language of norms

Social norms often function as a language through which people communicate values, intentions, character, status, or group membership.[1] This feature is particularly evident in what people choose to wear. Being correctly attired at a formal dinner party signals membership in an exclusive social group. Veiling serves as a symbol of a Muslim woman's adherence to traditional religious values. Choosing whether to wear a mask during the recent Covid epidemic was not just a response to a public health crisis, but acquired a political meaning: for some it expressed public-spiritedness while for others it represented undue interference by the state. As a result, non-maskers suffered significant social censure in some left-leaning communities, while in other communities non-masking was applauded as an assertion of individual liberty.

Behaviors that serve an economic purpose often acquire social significance as well. In the United States, tipping the waiter in a restaurant is an entrenched social norm that signals the patron's gratitude for good service; not doing so is considered stingy and invites the contempt of the server. In Japan, by contrast, tipping is considered a breach of decorum because it implies that the waiter needs to be paid in order to offer good service. More generally, the meaning of a social norm depends very much on social context, on where you are, who you are, and the nature of the interaction. The activities that norms support may be beneficial, harmful, or of little importance in themselves, but their violation can carry significant reputational penalties.

How do such behaviors take on particular meanings, and how do they coalesce into social norms? I argue that they evolve in much the same way that languages and dialects emerge from the repeated interactions of many individuals. The more often that a given behavior becomes imbued with a specific meaning, the stronger the incentive for each individual member of the group to follow it also, because deviations risk being misinterpreted. Over time, as

[1] For the role played by identity in economic decision-making see the pioneering work of Akerlof and Kranton 2000, 2010.

The Dynamics of Social Norms. H. Peyton Young, Oxford University Press.
 DOI: 10.1093/oso/9780198959052.003.0002

people interact, individual behaviors, expectations about others' behavior, and expectations about others' reactions to your own behavior, converge toward common understandings—a shared language that constitutes a social norm.[2]

2.2 Naming conventions: an experimental study

Subsequent chapters will illustrate this fundamental dynamic in different settings. Here I shall consider a seemingly simple case: the evolution of commonly accepted ways of naming people and objects. The game-theoretic analysis of this situation was initiated by David Lewis (1969), who argued that common knowledge and common beliefs are crucial for supporting signaling conventions as coordination equilibria. I shall argue that, as a practical matter, people can and do solve such coordination problems with very limited knowledge of the strategic environment in which they are embedded. In the next chapter I introduce a dynamic model that shows how such coordination is achieved through a decentralized process of learning and adaptation. Here I shall focus on one set of experiments that illustrates this type of adaptive process; still others are treated in Chapter 4.[3]

Let us represent the interaction structure of a society by a network in which each individual is located at a node, and two nodes are linked if and only if they communicate with one another. Figure 2.1 illustrates two distinct interaction networks. In the ring network, each individual interacts only with her nearest four neighbors (two on either side). In the complete network, everyone interacts with everyone else. Such structures represent the degree of mixing in the society.

Centola and Baronchelli (2015) conducted a series of online experiments in which subjects developed a common language for identifying specific individuals without any prior communication. Subjects were assigned to the nodes of a network but were not told what the network looked like. In each round, every subject was matched at random with one of its neighbors and they were shown a picture of a face (the same face was shown to all subjects). Each had to suggest a name for it without communicating with their partner. Neither of them was told the identity of their partner or their prior history of choices; all

[2] Similarly, among academics, the use of accepted terms of discourse and argumentation constitutes a social norm within the discipline that is crucial to communicating with one's peers and getting one's papers published.

[3] For recent theoretical work on the evolution of signaling conventions see Skyrms 2010, and Hutteger, Skyrms, Tarres, and Wagner 2014.

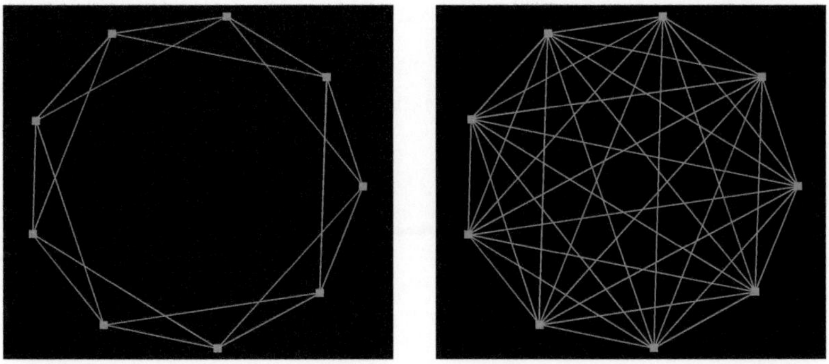

Figure 2.1 A ring network and a complete network.

they knew was the pattern of names that had been proposed by others with whom they were matched in prior encounters. The payoffs were as follows: if both members of a pair provided the same name, they earned a reward; otherwise they paid a small penalty. There was no restriction on the names that subjects could provide—that was left to their imagination. The network set-up mimicked real-life situations in which a sizable group of individuals interact randomly and some interactions are more likely than others, say because people live near each other, take similar transport to work, enjoy the same type of entertainment, are in the same profession, and so forth.

Over many plays of the game, subjects accumulated information about the names that were most popular among the people with whom they interacted. Based on this information, they tried to guess what name(s) would be most likely to match that of their current (anonymous) partner. The question is whether subjects' actual behavior led to stable "dialects," how long it took, and how the topology of the network shaped the distribution of emergent dialects.

Before discussing the results, let us observe that the emergence of different configurations depends crucially on the network topology. In a ring, for example, local "dialects" tend to coalesce quite rapidly, and can be sustained (at least temporarily) because members of a local group interact mainly with each other. In a complete network, by contrast, it is difficult for a small subgroup to coordinate on any one term because its members interact mainly with outsiders. Hence when a language convention emerges it will be global rather than local.

This prediction is borne out by the experimental results. Figure 2.2 (top panel) shows a representative evolutionary path for a ring network with 24 agents. By round 10, several distinct local dialects have emerged in which small groups of nearby agents choose the same name. Altogether there are

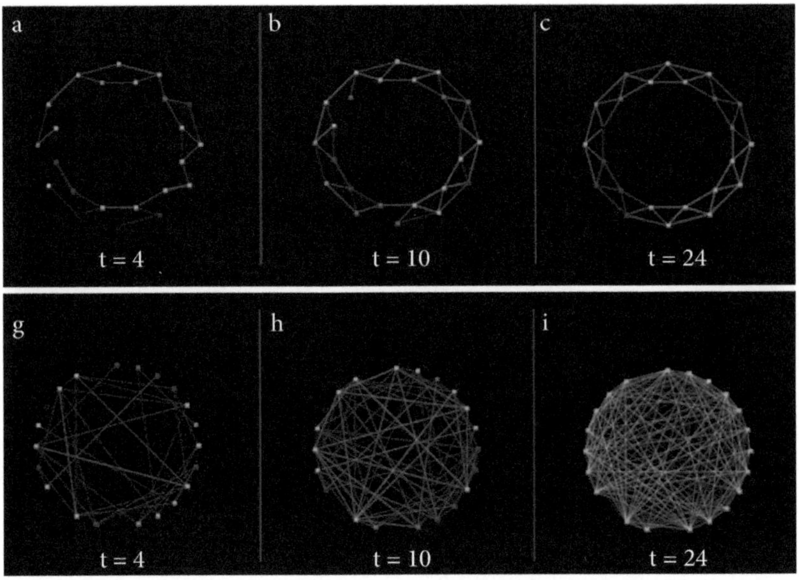

Figure 2.2 The Name Game. An edge is colored if the two subjects proposed the same name in their most recent match; otherwise it is white. Top panel: ring network. Bottom panel: complete network.

Source: Figure 2 in Centola and Baronchelli 2015, "The spontaneous emergence of conventions: an experimental study of cultural evolution," *Proceedings of the National Academy of Sciences* 112(7): 1989–1994.

five dialects with contested border regions separating them, and they remain intact for quite a few periods. The bottom panel of Figure 2.2 shows a representative path for the complete graph. Compared to the ring network, there are more failures to coordinate in the initial rounds, but by round 10 a dominant convention has become established, and by round 24 this convention has displaced all of the others.

More generally, these experiments show that norms, whether local or global, can emerge endogenously by a bottom-up process in which subjects adjust their behavior through a trial-and-error learning process. It is not necessary for them to know anything about the overall structure of the network or their own position in it. Shared meanings emerge purely due to positive feedback effects, and do not pre-suppose common knowledge of the evolutionary process, or more than elementary levels of rationality on the part of the subjects.

The experiments cited above are of course very much simplified compared to the processes by which norms, and the meanings attached to them, evolve in practice. Indeed, while the experiments are concerned with the way that subjects coordinate on a specific way of referring to an object (a pointer), it does not explore the norms that emerge around the *right way* to refer to an object or situation. In practice, however, terms of reference can become imbued with connotations and meanings that go way beyond their function as pointers, and that can have quite negative implications for those who misuse them. These norms of usage can evolve quite rapidly. The current use of certain four-letter words would have been completely unacceptable in polite discourse a generation ago. Some ways of referring to racial and ethnic groups that used to be commonplace are now considered taboo.

More generally, norms of usage, and responses to their infraction, are constantly evolving through a mostly bottom-up process of individual interactions and discussions, just as language itself evolves. My contention is that many other norms can be seen in a similar light: they amount to complex forms of communication that signal group membership or identity, and their violation can have significant reputational repercussions. In the remainder of this chapter, I shall briefly discuss three examples of such norms that have undergone major shifts over a relatively short period of time, and that illustrate how these shifts can be understood in terms of cumulative reinforcement through social interactions.

2.3 Formal attire: tux or tails?

Norms of attire for formal occasions are a key indicator of social class. These norms are constantly evolving and keeping abreast of them is part of the signaling game. A case in point is formal evening attire for men. Although the current standard is black tie (or tuxedo), this was not always the case. In fact, when it was first introduced in the late nineteenth century, the tuxedo amounted to a form of "dressing down" that would have been considered out of place at formal evening events, where the established norm was white tie and tailcoat.[4] The shift from full evening dress to short coat and black tie occurred gradually over several decades in the late nineteenth century. It first appeared among some members of the English aristocracy, who found wearing a short coat more convenient at weekend house parties on their country estates. It was given a boost by Edward Prince of Wales (the future King Edward VII), who ordered a blue silk smoking jacket from his Savile Row tailor Henry Poole & Co. for use at dinner parties at his Sandringham estate. In 1886 the new style crossed the Atlantic due to a court visit by a wealthy American, James Brown

[4] The following account is based on "Black Tie and Tuxedo History," Chapter 3 in Gentlemansgazette.com/tuxedo-black-tie-guide, 2018.

Potter and his actress wife Cora. The Prince invited the couple to dinner at Sandringham, and when Mr. Potter asked his host for advice on what to wear for such an occasion, the Prince referred him to his tailor to be fitted for a short evening jacket. Mr. Potter then brought the innovation back home to Tuxedo Park, an exclusive residential community for prominent New Yorkers. The new mode of dress gradually spread to others in their social circle, and became known as the tuxedo.

The process by which the tux became the new norm illustrates the interplay between top-down and bottom-up influences that can be seen in many cases. Initially it gained legitimacy within a social group because of its adoption by a prestigious member of that group, who presumably had nothing to lose by disregarding current convention (unlike Obama, who had to worry about the reaction of voters when he failed to wear a flag lapel pin). The new way of dressing then crossed the ocean due to a chance encounter at a dinner party, and subsequently gained a foothold within an exclusive social group in New York. This is also a common pattern in the evolution of social norms: it is easier for a new norm to take root within a small group of closely linked individuals than to be adopted all at once by a large diffuse group; once it is safely established within the small group, the norm can then diffuse more widely.

2.4 Gender norms and roller bags

The roller bag is a simple and practical idea that was first patented in 1972 by Bernard Sadow.[5] However, he had great difficulty persuading anyone to produce and market it, largely because firms feared that men would be reluctant to adopt it due to its perceived "femininity." Moreover, this prediction turned out to be correct. The implication of rolling a bag is that you are too weak to carry it: it isn't macho. Even after roller bags became available, they were largely shunned by men (in some cases men would insist on carrying rather than rolling them). Instead, they gained an initial foothold among airline stewardesses, which solidified their feminine connotations even more. Nevertheless, the norm eventually shifted, presumably because some men found the ease of use outweighed any negative implications about their masculinity; indeed it seems plausible that the early adopters were precisely those with the greatest self-confidence in their masculinity. Gradually, through a process

[5] In its more modern form (with retractable handle) the concept was patented in 1987 by Robert Plath, a pilot at Northwest Airlines (Goldstein 2019).

of social diffusion, roller bags became more and more common until their gendered connotation virtually disappeared.

A similar story can be told for the choice of career.[6] The more that a specific subgroup is represented in a given profession (by ethnicity, race, gender, or social class), the more the choice of that profession is deemed "normal" or "appropriate" for that subgroup (and less appropriate for others), due to its reinforcement of norms of identity. For example, if the great majority of hospital nurses (or typists or airline stewardesses or telephone operators) are female, or the great majority of engineers (or truck drivers or construction workers or doctors) are male, career choice becomes invested with significance regarding one's sexual identity, and is not motivated entirely by one's personal desire to pursue a given profession. Similarly, going into investment banking (or law or medicine), is the norm within some social groups, whereas opening a plumbing business or a car dealership or a construction firm will be viewed as less prestigious (even though these careers may lead to higher lifetime incomes).

2.5 Tipping

Tipping is a social norm that varies substantially among different countries. Travel guides devote considerable space to describing what is expected in various situations for travelers who are anxious to avoid giving offense. Different norms may apply to restaurant waiters, taxi drivers, porters, barbers, hairdressers, tour guides, hotel staff, and so on. Each group expects to receive a percentage of the bill whose size depends on local custom. In the United States the customary tip for restaurant waiters used to be 15% but recently there has been a trend toward 20% and even larger amounts. In many other countries, a fixed service charge is added to the bill and no specific tip is expected over and above that amount. Nevertheless, customers often do leave a little extra, or they round the bill up to a whole number, a courtesy to the waiter that (in a cash economy) simplifies the problem of making change.

Tipping originated as a way of expressing appreciation for assistance rendered to guests by household servants.[7] In England, for example, guests at

[6] In some cases career choices were effectively closed to one gender or another due to outright discrimination. I am focusing here on the "representativeness" effect that lingers even when there are no direct impediments to choosing a given profession (Carvalho and Pradelski 2022, 2024). For a general theory of how identities are constructed and how they affect economic decisions see Akerlof and Kranton 2000, 2010.

[7] The following account is based on Segrave 2009.

a country house would customarily leave small gratuities for the household help. It was a distinctly class-based transaction expressing a relationship of dependency between master and servant. Beginning in the second half of the nineteenth century, well-heeled American travelers to Europe brought the tipping custom back home, and it gradually began to spread. However, initially there was strong resistance in some quarters, as tipping was viewed by many as redolent of class distinctions and inappropriate for a democratic society. *The New York Times* opined that "American workingmen should not accept gratuities. They have their citizenship, independence, and every opportunity to rise in the world." In the early twentieth century there were numerous attempts to ban the practice: anti-tipping legislation was enacted in six states: Arkansas, Iowa, Mississippi, Tennessee, South Carolina, and Washington State. These fizzled out in part because local laws and norms were undermined by travelers who were unfamiliar with them.

Thus, despite being initially reviled as an expression of class distinctions, tipping has now become solidly entrenched in the United States, indeed much more so than in most European countries. It provides people with an opportunity to be in control of a situation and to reward the perceived quality of someone else's performance. It also reflects the widespread belief that people need to be incentivized with money payments to do a good job—witness the bonus culture in American business. (Whether such norms actually have the intended motivational effect is open to dispute.)

More generally, tipping is not solely an arms-length economic transaction; it has a sociological dimension that expresses the relationship between patron and client, between server and served. The incentive to follow the norm arises from the interpretation of the action in comparison to what others are doing. Its meaning is relative rather absolute. The manner in which such norms become established (and occasionally change) occurs mostly through bottom-up, piecemeal decisions by many dispersed individuals, although the process may sometimes be given a boost by organized campaigns (such as the recent promotion of higher tips for waiters on the grounds that they are poorly paid).

In the following chapters I introduce a model that can help us understand more generally how norms become established, how norm shifts occur, why they persist even though (in some cases) everyone would be better off if they were abandoned, and what types of interventions might be most effective in changing them.

3

Norm Dynamics: Theory

3.1 A model of norm dynamics

This chapter introduces a simple but versatile model that captures the dynamics of norms in a general setting. The key driver is the desire to coordinate one's actions with the actions of others. The more people who do x, the greater the propensity to do x too. The more people who tip 20% in a restaurant, the less comfortable I feel about tipping 15%. The more people in the audience who give the orchestra a standing ovation, the more I am inclined to stand up too, lest the performers think I didn't much like it. The more often US politicians wear a flag lapel pin, the greater the reputational cost of not wearing one. The more families in a Somalian village who circumcise their daughters, the more likely it is that an uncircumcised daughter will not find social acceptance or a suitable marriage partner. The more common it is to be divorced, the less stigma is attached to getting a divorce. In short, the perceived benefit from taking a given action (or the cost of not taking it) increases with its prevalence in a given reference group.

The motives and mechanisms that generate this feedback loop vary from one case to another; in fact, multiple mechanisms are often at work simultaneously. Volunteering for a neighborhood clean-up may be motivated by wanting a tidier environment, but it may also result from the fear of being considered irresponsible by one's neighbors if one fails to volunteer. Standing ovations are a way of communicating strong approval of a performance, but there is also a physical coordination motive: if most people are standing one cannot see the stage without standing up too. We can formalize such feedback effects by a model that embodies the individual benefits or costs from an activity as well as the social benefits or costs that accrue from the actions of others. The model is simple but leads to a surprisingly rich array of dynamical behaviors, as we shall see in due course.

Consider a group of m individuals, each of whom can take an action in some set X. A *state* is an m-vector $\boldsymbol{x} = (x_1, x_2, \ldots, x_m)$, where x_i denotes the current choice of action by player i. In some settings the set of actions will be dichotomous—standing or sitting at the end of a performance, wearing a flag

The Dynamics of Social Norms. H. Peyton Young, Oxford University Press.
 DOI: 10.1093/oso/9780198959052.003.0003

lapel pin, enlisting in the military, using a carry bag or a roller bag, having a child out of wedlock, getting a divorce. In other settings there is a range of possible actions: how much to tip a waiter, how much commission to pay a hedge fund manager, how severely to circumcise one's daughter, how much to contribute to a school fundraiser, how many hours to spend tending the common garden, and so forth. In the interest of simplicity, I shall focus here on the dichotomous case; later chapters will extend the approach to situations with more than two alternatives.

Each individual's utility is a function of his own action and the actions taken by others. The *private* utility to i from taking action x_i will be denoted by $u_i(x_i)$. The *social utility to i* from interacting with some agent $j \neq i$ is given by $\lambda s_{ij}(x_i, x_j)$ where λ is a real-valued scaling parameter. I shall assume that social and private utilities are additive, so that the total payoff to i in state $\boldsymbol{x}$ is

$$U_i(\boldsymbol{x}) = u_i(x_i) + \lambda \sum_{j \neq i} s_{ij}(x_i, x_j) + \varepsilon_i(\boldsymbol{x}), \tag{1}$$

where $\varepsilon_i(\boldsymbol{x})$ is a random variable (a payoff shock).[1]

Although the form of the social interaction term $s_{ij}(x_i, x_j)$ varies from one situation to another, my focus here will be on cases where the interactions have a common payoff structure and are weighted according to the social or geographical proximity of the agents, that is, there is a function $s\colon X^2 \to R$ and nonnegative *weights* w_{ij} such that $s_{ij}(x_i, x_j) = w_{ij}s(x_i, x_j)$.

Suppose, for the moment, that there are no payoff shocks. A *global norm* is a Nash equilibrium of the game defined by (1) in which everyone plays the same action. When agents are embedded in a social network, there will often exist equilibria in which everyone in a given "neighborhood" plays the same action, but not everyone plays the same action globally. These are *local* or *regional norms*. There may also exist equilibria in which most agents play the same action, but a few do not because their private utility outweighs the benefit from conforming to their neighbors. I shall refer to these as *quasi-norms.* These variants arise naturally in applications, as we shall see in due course.

3.2 Local conformity and global diversity

The social interactions model has surprisingly rich implications that set it apart from situations where social interactions are not present. The first point

[1] The microfoundations of this representation are analyzed by Root and Sadler 2026.

to emphasize is that norms tend to mask or suppress heterogeneity in agents' private utilities, due to the benefits from coordinating with others (the *compression effect*). Secondly, norms may differ between regions or subgroups due to a different distribution of preferences within these groups, and/or to different evolutionary paths of development. These twin phenomena—*local conformity* and *global diversity*—are a characteristic feature of social norms that can be tested empirically.

To illustrate, consider a pure coordination game with two actions (A and B) in which a pair of interacting agents will each receive a positive payoff if they play the same action and zero otherwise. If the population is composed of distinct subgroups or "villages" that do not interact at all, distinct norms may take root in different villages, leading to substantial diversity globally but complete conformity locally.

Less obviously, much the same thing can happen when agents are not in isolated villages but are distributed more or less evenly across the landscape, as in Figure 3.1. Suppose that coordinated actions by the members of an adjacent

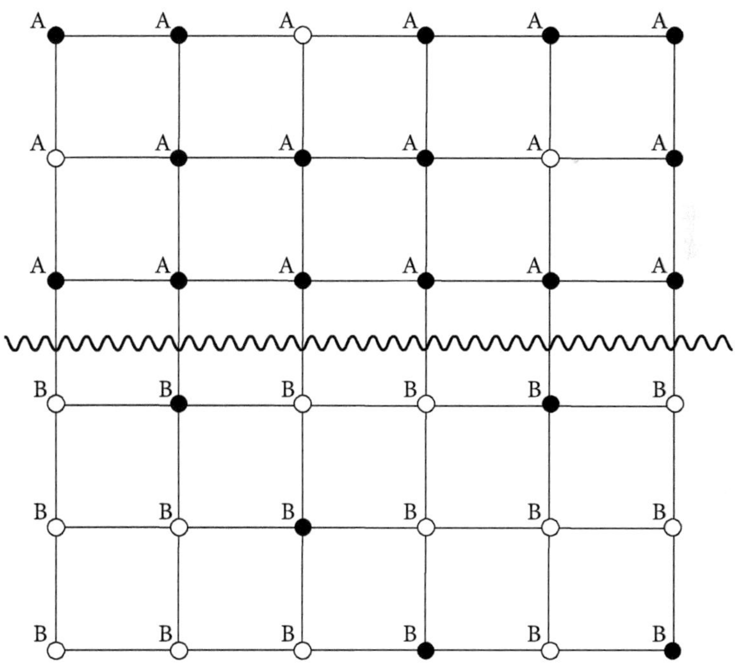

Figure 3.1 An example illustrating regional norms. Payoffs equal 1 for coordinating with a neighbor, 0 for miscoordinating. Agents at hollow nodes have a private payoff of 1 from B and 0 from A; the reverse holds for agents at solid nodes.

pair lead to a payoff of 1 for each, whereas uncoordinated actions result in a payoff of 0. Suppose further that agents at hollow nodes have a private payoff of 1 from B and 0 from A, whereas the reverse holds for agents at solid nodes. The state in Figure 3.1 constitutes an equilibrium that demonstrates local conformity and global diversity: in spite of heterogeneity within each region, action A is the norm in the North and B is the norm in the South. No one (even at the border between regions) has an incentive to switch. In the absence of social interactions, the outcome would be a mixture of As and Bs in each region, with A predominant in the North and B predominant in the South. The presence of social interactions suppresses individual differences due to the benefits of coordinating with one's neighbors, and leads to regional norms. A particular consequence is that individuals with identical private preferences may behave very differently if they live in different regions. This is the *excess diversity* effect.

Next let us consider a variant of this example in which only one of the actions—say B—has private costs, whereas A has none. For example, B could represent footbinding or dueling. In the absence of social interactions, everyone would choose A. In the presence of social interactions, the benefit from conforming to one's neighbors may outweigh the private cost of the harmful action due to negative reputational effects. As before, let us assume that the coordination benefits are 1 for each member of a linked pair. Assume further that at each solid node the private cost of B equals 1/2, whereas at each hollow node the private cost of B equals 5 (see Figure 3.2). Under these conditions no one has an incentive to switch from B to A or vice versa, hence this configuration is a pure equilibrium consisting of two local norms and a quasi-norm with three isolates.

Local conformity and global diversity are general features of social interactions that arise under many alternative specifications of the model. For example, the social disutility from choosing an action might increase as the square of the proportion choosing the opposite action. Social disutility may also be stronger in one direction than another: wearing a flag lapel pin when most others don't wear one may be viewed as an unimportant personal choice, whereas not wearing a flag lapel pin when most others do can pose a serious risk to a politician's reputation. Asymmetries in the direction and/or extent of deviations from a norm have important implications for the dynamics of adjustment, as we shall see in Chapter 7.[2]

In general, whenever there is an incentive to coordinate with others, interacting individuals will tend to behave similarly even though they have different

[2] See Akerlof 1997, Durlauf 1997, Brock and Durlauf 2001, Blume and Durlauf 2003.

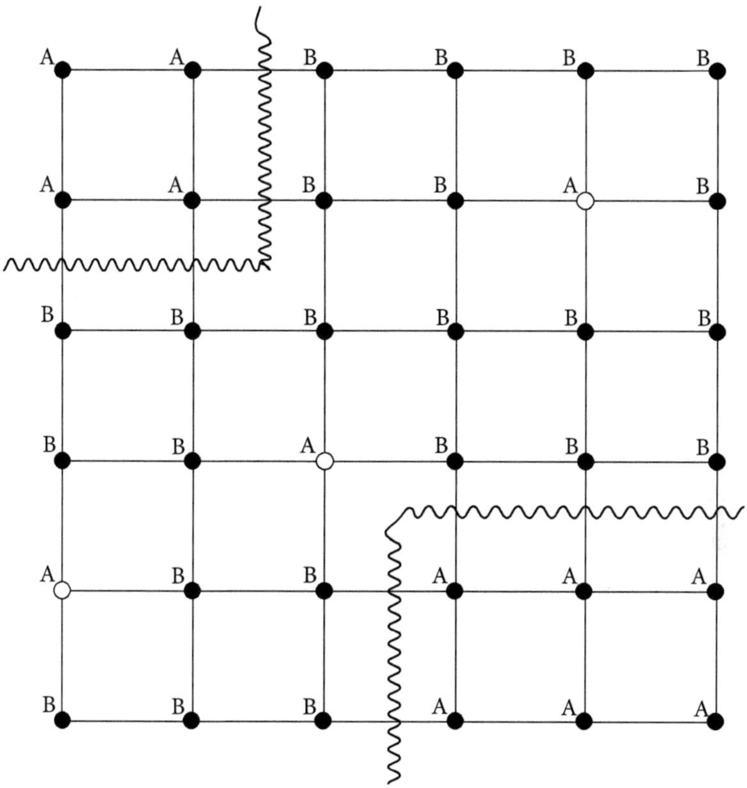

Figure 3.2 An example illustrating two regional norms and one quasi-norm. Payoffs equal 1 for coordinating with a neighbor, 0 for miscoordinating. The private cost of B equals 1/2 at solid nodes and 5 at hollow nodes. The private cost of A is zero for everyone.

preferences, and non-interacting individuals may behave differently even though they have similar preferences. Empirical studies of this "neighborhood effect" have been conducted for a wide variety of behaviors, including dropping out of school, having children out of wedlock, and engaging in criminal activity.[3] The empirical challenge is to control for omitted variables that lead to positive correlation in behaviors but do not result from social interactions. For example, people may choose to live close to those who have similar preferences to themselves (homophily), in which case similarity in behaviors results from similarity in preferences rather than conformity per se.

[3] See among others Crane 1991, Case and Katz 1991, Akerlof et al. 1996, Glaeser, Sacerdote, and Scheinkman 1996, Glaeser and Scheinkman 2001.

In Chapter 6, I shall discuss a setting where some of these confounding effects can be controlled for, namely, contractual terms between landlords and tenants in US agriculture. It turns out that contractual terms are strikingly uniform within particular geographical regions, but differ markedly across regions, even though there is a substantial and observable degree of heterogeneity within each region (notably, local differences in soil quality). Furthermore, the data are sufficiently detailed that one can examine whether this "compression effect" due to local norms distorts the competitive returns to labor and land that would be expected if social interaction effects were not present, and it turns out that the distortions are substantial.

3.3 Stochastic norm dynamics: the tipping game

The existence of multiple equilibria in social interactions models would seem to imply a fundamental lack of predictability: idiosyncratic initial conditions might lead to radically different and inherently unpredictable outcomes due to path dependency and lock-in effects. When random perturbations are incorporated into the evolutionary process, there is unpredictability in the short run, but in the long run some equilibria are more likely to emerge than others independently of initial conditions. Thus the process may actually become *more predictable* when random perturbations are present, because initial conditions and path-dependency effects are washed out in the long run. The result is a dynamic model of equilibrium selection.[4]

The basic idea can be illustrated by an everyday example. Suppose that I have just finished eating in a restaurant and the waiter has presented me with the bill. How much tip should I leave? The answer depends on where I am. In Japan, I would not be expected to leave anything; indeed, tipping would be considered out of place. In Europe, I might leave a small extra amount in addition to the standard service charge. In the United States, the traditional tip used to be 15%, but in recent years it has been ratcheting up to 20%, 25%, and beyond, spurred on by the trend for restaurants to "suggest" various percentages when paying the bill. Whatever the local custom may be, if I give less than is usual and expected the waiter may feel offended; moreover, I may think the worse of myself for being stingy. If I leave more than is customary,

[4] This approach stands in contrast to that of Harsanyi and Selten (1988) who argue that some equilibrium outcomes are inherently more plausible than others. In some cases, the two approaches yield similar predictions, namely, the selection of risk-dominant equilibria in symmetric 2×2 coordination games.

I will be the poorer but the waiter will no doubt be grateful and I will probably be pleased with my show of generosity. Note that, in either case, there need be no direct interaction with other diners (assuming that I am dining alone). Rather, my utility depends on my own (and the waiter's) knowledge of how my action *relates* to the actions of others in the relevant community.

To illustrate with a simple case, suppose that there are just two salient choices, High tip (H) and Low tip (L). Tipping H costs 3 while tipping L costs 1. The level of service is provided up-front, and is not conditional on the forthcoming tip. (I assume that there is no repeated relationship, which would change the incentives substantially.) However, there are social/psychological payoffs even in a one-shot interaction. In particular, tipping L when everyone else is tipping H makes me look stingy and will probably offend the waiter. This has a psychological cost of *s*. Tipping H when everyone else is tipping L may earn some extra gratitude from the waiter, or perhaps just a warm glow from feeling generous, which has a psychological benefit of *g*. These considerations lead to a game with the following structure:[5]

The Tipping Game

Others' actions

		H	L	
Own action	H	$-3,\ -3$	$-3+g,\ -1-s$	(2)
	L	$-1-s,\ -3+g$	$-1,\ -1$	

Let us assume that LL and HH are coordination equilibria, which holds when $g < 2 < s$, that is, the warm glow is not too great, and the stigma from being seen as stingy is not too small.

Consider the dynamic process in which one diner is chosen at random from the population, and she chooses how much to tip given her current assessment of how much others are tipping, that is, the proportions choosing H or L. Let p be the proportion of others who choose H. Then her payoff from choosing H equals $-3 + (1 - p)g$, whereas her payoff from L equals $-1 - ps$. Her estimate of p may be based on personal experience, asking around, reading tourist guidebooks, or some combination thereof. Whatever the source, there will almost inevitably be some error in assessing the true state. Furthermore, even if she does know the true state, she may deviate from choosing a best response depending on her mood, the actual quality of service

[5] To put the payoffs in the format of expression (1), let $u(H) = -3$, $u(L) = -1$, $s(H, L) = g$, $s(L, H) = s$, $s(H, H) = s(L, L) = 0$, and $\lambda = 1/(m - 1)$.

that day, and other idiosyncratic factors. Thus, we can think of the dynamics as a stochastic process in which people revise their actions from time to time, and usually (but not always) choose a best response to the current state.

What is the long-run behavior of such a process? To analyze this issue, let us suppose that the current state is a norm, say all-L. To displace it requires that the proportion p^* or more of the others in the population switch to H, where $p^* = (2 - g)/(s - g)$.[6] (Recall our assumption that $g < 2 < s$.) Once this happens, H becomes a best response. Until that point is reached, however, each switch by some individual has a low probability, because it represents a non-best response to the current state. (To be concrete, we can think of each non-best response as having some small probability $\varepsilon > 0$.) Similarly, to displace the norm all-H requires that at least $1 - p^*$ of the other players choose L. Displacing all-L is easier than displacing all-H when $p^* < 1/2$, that is, when $g + s > 4$. Displacing all-H is easier when $p^* > 1/2$, that is, $g + s < 4$. In the latter case L is said to be "risk-dominant," whereas in the former case H is risk-dominant. In the long run, as the process shifts back and forth between the two equilibria, the risk-dominant equilibrium is the most likely one to occur. It can be shown that when the probability of choosing a non-best reply is very small, the risk-dominant equilibrium occurs, over the long run, with probability close to one. Note that risk dominance is not necessarily the same as payoff dominance: in this example the H-norm is payoff inferior (from the diners' standpoint), but it may be risk-dominant. The connection between risk dominance and stochastic stability will be explored in detail in Sections 3.6 and 3.7.[7]

Of course, when the relevant population is large and the probability of non-best responses is small, the transition probabilities between equilibria will be very small, and one may question whether this analysis is meaningful. The answer is that this situation should be viewed as a *limiting case* for which tight results can be formulated. As will be seen in the next chapter, experiments show that deviations from best response actually occur quite frequently; moreover, they tend to occur more frequently the smaller is the payoff loss associated with the deviation. In this case, transitions between equilibria may actually occur quite rapidly, as will be shown in Chapter 5.

[6] The minimum number of agents who must switch to H is the least integer $k^* \geq \frac{2-g}{s-g}(m-1)$.

[7] The current effort by restaurants to shift the tipping percentage upward focusses on manipulating s by claiming that waiters are poorly paid, thus making diners feel guilty if they don't leave a generous tip. This example highlights the potential for manipulating a norm's meaning in order to induce a norm shift, a tactic that we shall see employed in many other settings.

The preceding analysis of tipping norms is very much simplified in order to make certain basic points about the role played by stochastic variation in the transition between norms. A more realistic analysis would have to include more than two levels of tip. Although in principle there is a continuum of possible choices, in practice only a few percentages will be perceived as salient. In this case the analysis of the dynamics becomes more complex, but the essential idea is similar to the 2×2 case. Namely, one computes the probability of transiting between each pair of equilibria when the probability of choosing a non-best reply is small, and from these pairwise transition probabilities one can deduce the equilibrium that is most likely to occur in the long run. This approach will be illustrated in Section 3.5.

Another complicating factor is that the level of service may adjust over time to the prevailing tipping norm. For example, if people are expected to tip more, restaurants may be able to attract more competent staff, which leads to a higher level of service. In other words, there is a potential interaction between norms of tipping and standards of service that one could examine in a more complex version of the model presented above.

3.4 A general model of stochastic norm dynamics

Let us now step back from particular examples and formulate a model of norm dynamics in more general terms. Consider a population of m agents and a finite action space X. Time periods are discrete. The *state* at the end of period t is an m-vector $\boldsymbol{x}^t$, where $x_i^t \in X$ is the current choice of action by player i. At the start of period $t + 1$, one agent, say i, is selected at random. With high probability she chooses an action x_i that maximizes the deterministic part of her utility function, and with low probability other actions are chosen due to such factors as idiosyncratic utility shocks, misperceptions, and experimentation.

In the evolutionary games literature, there are two standard models of perturbed best response behavior. The *uniform error model* posits that every non-best response is chosen with a small positive error rate ε.[8] This is the model we considered in our analysis of the tipping game. An alternative approach is to suppose that an agent's utility for each action is perturbed by random shocks, and the agent maximizes utility subject to these shocks. A common assumption is that the shocks are i.i.d. extreme-value distributed,

[8] The uniform error model was introduced in this setting by Kandori, Mailath, and Rob 1993 and Young 1993a.

in which case the response function has a logit format.[9] Namely, if the state in period t is $\boldsymbol{x}^t$, and if i revises in period $t + 1$, then for some nonnegative real number β (called the *response parameter*), the probability that she chooses action x is

$$P[x_i^{t+1} = x] = e^{\beta U_i(x, \boldsymbol{x}_{-i}^t)} \Big/ \sum_{y \in X} e^{\beta U_i(y, \boldsymbol{x}_{-i}^t)}. \tag{3}$$

(Here $\boldsymbol{x}_{-i}^t$ denotes the actions of agents other than i.) The larger the value of β, the more likely the agent is to choose an action that maximizes the deterministic part of the utility function. Note that, unlike the uniform error model, the probability of deviating from best-reply behavior decreases as the prospective loss in payoff increases. This property seems intuitively reasonable; moreover it is supported by the experimental behavior of laboratory subjects, as we shall see in Chapter 4. Payoff-dependent errors can also lead to much faster transitions between equilibria than do uniform errors, as will be shown in Chapter 5.

In general, a distribution of perturbation probabilities yields a stochastic dynamic process whose behavior can be analyzed using the theory of large deviations in Markov chains. Under very general conditions, the process will have a unique long-run (ergodic) distribution, which represents the probability that each state is visited over long periods of time independently of the initial state.[10] When deviations from best reply have sufficiently low probability, the long-run distribution will typically be highly concentrated on a unique state (or a small subset of states), which are said to be *stochastically stable*.[11]

3.5 Tipping revisited

For a given perturbation distribution, the computation of the stochastically stable states relies on the concept of "resistance" to transiting between equilibria. The approach is best illustrated by considering a concrete example, namely the tipping game with three levels of tip—High, Medium, and Low—and

[9] This is a standard model in the discrete-choice literature (McFadden 1974). Its application to equilibrium selection in games was pioneered by Blume 1993.

[10] For example, the long-run distribution exists and is unique if the state space is finite, the perturbation probabilities are time-invariant, and every state can be reached from every other state by a path having positive probability.

[11] This concept was introduced as an equilibrium selection criterion by Foster and Young 1990. A general method for computing the stochastically stable states is given in Young 1993a.

errors that are uniformly distributed. To avoid cumbersome notation, I shall ignore "warm glow" payoffs and focus on the role of stigma from tipping too little. Consider the following payoff matrix:

$$\begin{array}{ccccc} & & \multicolumn{3}{c}{\text{Others' actions}} \\ & & H & M & L \\ & H & -3,-3 & -3,-2-s & -3,-1-s' \\ \text{Own actions} & M & -2-s,-3 & -2,-2 & -2,-1-s \\ & L & -1-s',-3 & -1-s,-2 & -1,-1 \end{array} \quad (4)$$

Here s represents the stigma from tipping somewhat less than the current norm, while $s' > s$ represents the stigma from tipping much less. When $s > 1$ and $s' > 2$, we obtain a coordination game with three strict pure equilibria.

Suppose that every deviation from best response occurs with some small probability $\varepsilon > 0$. The minimum number of deviations required to transit from a given equilibrium to another is called the *resistance* of the transition. For example, let k_{LM} denote the minimum number of deviations needed to transit from the L-norm to the M-norm. This is the minimum number of M-players needed to make M a best response when the remainder of the population plays L. In a population of size m, k_{LM} is the smallest integer k such that $-1 - s(k/(m-1)) \le -2$, that is, $k/(m-1) \ge 1/s$. When m is not too small, the resistance is more or less proportional (subject to rounding) to the smallest *proportion* of others in the population needed to shift the process from one equilibrium to another. These proportions are called *relative resistances* and are shown in Table 3.1.

Now consider a graph with three vertices labeled L, M, H. A *rooted tree* consists of two directed edges such that all paths lead to the same vertex (the root). For each possible root (L, M, H) there are three rooted trees. The *resistance of a tree* is the sum of the resistances on its edges. It can be shown that *an equilibrium is stochastically stable if and only if it corresponds to the root of a tree*

Table 3.1 Relative resistances of transitions between equilibria in the 3 × 3 tipping game

$r_{LM} = 1/s,$	$r_{ML} = 1 - 1/s$
$r_{MH} = 1/s,$	$r_{HM} = 1 - 1/s$
$r_{LH} = 2/s',$	$r_{HL} = 1 - 2/s'$

L → M → H	M → L → H	M → H, L → H
1/3 1/3	2/3 2/5	1/3 2/5
L → H → M	H → L → M	L → M, H → M
2/5 2/3	3/5 1/3	1/3 2/3
H → M → L	M → H → L	M → L, H → L
2/3 2/3	1/3 3/5	2/3 3/5

Figure 3.3 Rooted trees and relative resistances when $s = 3$ and $s' = 5$.

with minimum resistance.[12] When the population is reasonably large, the relative resistances are nearly proportional to the resistances and yield essentially the same result.

To illustrate, choose $s = 3$ and $s' = 5$. The relative resistances of all nine rooted trees are shown in Figure 3.3. The minimum occurs for the tree with root H and edges L → M and M → H. It follows that the H norm is stochastically stable, that is, H is by far the most likely level of tip when the error rate ε is sufficiently small. Moreover, the structure of the minimum resistance rooted tree shows that the most likely transition from L to H occurs via the intermediate action M. This stepwise transition structure occurs in other applications, as will be shown in Chapter 7.

The rooted trees approach to computing the stochastically stable states is very general and can be applied to many other situations, including games with a large number of equilibria and/or perturbation distributions that are not uniform. However, the concept of "resistance" must be adapted to the specific distribution at hand. To illustrate, consider the logit model with response parameter β. When β is large, $e^{-\beta}$ is very small and the probability of choosing a non-best reply with payoff loss Λ (relative to a best response) is approximately $e^{-\beta\Lambda}$. In this case, Λ is the "resistance" of the one-step transition, and the resistance of a path from one equilibrium to another is the sum of the payoff losses along the path (not offsetting them by payoff gains). To find the stochastically stable equilibrium in this case, one finds the least-resistant path

[12] This result holds provided that the unperturbed best-response process converges almost surely to a pure Nash equilibrium from any initial state, i.e., the game is "weakly acyclic" (Young 1993a). This is the case for the tipping game.

from every equilibrium to every other equilibrium using the sum-of-losses definition of resistance. The rooted tree with minimum total resistance has the stochastically stable equilibrium as its root.[13]

A limitation of this approach is that it only identifies the most likely equilibria when the probability of non-best responses is very small. It is an open problem to derive general conditions under which this method identifies the most likely equilibria even when the perturbations are not especially small. There is, however, a class of games and perturbations for which this problem has a particularly simple and elegant solution, as will be shown next.

3.6 Equilibrium selection in potential games

Consider a situation where agents are located at the nodes of an undirected network, and each agent can choose an action in the finite set X. Suppose that the payoff is 1 for coordinating with each neighbor, and 0 for mis-coordinating. The payoff to agent i in state $\boldsymbol{x}$ is his private payoff $u_i(x_i)$ plus the number of his neighbors who also choose x_i. Let $c(\boldsymbol{x})$ denote the number of coordinated pairs and let $\rho(\boldsymbol{x}) = c(\boldsymbol{x}) + \sum_i u_i(x_i)$.

Suppose, for the moment, that there are no perturbations in the players' payoff functions. Consider the dynamic process in which one player is selected at random in each period and is given an opportunity to revise her action. She switches if and only if there exists an action that represents a *strict* payoff improvement given what others are doing in the current state. If the process starts in an arbitrary state $\boldsymbol{x}$ that is not an equilibrium, then there is at least one agent, say i, who can strictly improve her payoff, and there is a positive probability that this agent will revise next period. The resulting change in her payoff equals the change in the number of coordinated edges plus the change in her private payoff. In other words, *the change in her payoff equals the change in* $\rho(\boldsymbol{x})$. It follows that, given any disequilibrium state, there is a positive probability that next period the function $\rho(\boldsymbol{x})$ will increase by an amount that is bounded away from zero. (If someone is chosen who cannot improve her payoff, the state remains the same and $\rho(\boldsymbol{x})$ does not change.) Since the state space is finite, the process will almost surely reach a state from which $\rho(\boldsymbol{x})$ cannot increase any further, hence it constitutes a Nash equilibrium.

[13] A formal definition of resistance for more general perturbation distributions is given in Young 1993a.

The function $\rho(\boldsymbol{x})$ is called a *potential function*, and the corresponding game is a *potential game*.[14] This class of games is surprisingly general and arises in many applications, as we shall see in later chapters. To state the concept more generally, recall that the deterministic part of the payoff functions takes the form

$$U_i(\boldsymbol{x}) = u_i(x_i) + \lambda \sum_j w_{ij} s(x_i, x_j). \tag{5}$$

The payoffs define a *potential game* if there is a function $\rho^* : X^n \to R$ such that a unilateral change of action by any player changes the revising player's payoff by the corresponding change in potential, that is,

$$\forall i, x_i, x'_i, \boldsymbol{x}_{-i}, \rho^*(x_i, \boldsymbol{x}_{-i}) - \rho^*\left(x'_i, \boldsymbol{x}_{-i}\right) = U_i\left(x_i, \boldsymbol{x}_{-i}\right) - U_i\left(x'_i, \boldsymbol{x}_{-i}\right). \tag{6}$$

A particular case arises when the influence weights w_{ij} are symmetric ($w_{ij} = w_{ji}$ for all i and j), and the *two-person* game defined by $s(x_i, x_j)$ is a potential game with potential function $\rho : X^2 \to R$. In this case the m-person social interactions game also has a potential function, namely,

$$\rho^*(\boldsymbol{x}) = \sum_i u_i(x_i) + \lambda \sum_i \sum_{j \geq i} w_{ij} \rho(x_i, x_j). \tag{7}$$

Such a representation arises whenever the two-person game is symmetric and each player has just two actions. To see why, let us write the payoffs from a symmetric 2×2 game as follows:

	A	B
A	a, a	d, c
B	c, d	b, b

(8)

This is a coordination game if $a > c$ and $b > d$. Consider the function

$$\rho(A, A) = a - c, \rho(B, B) = b - d, \rho(A, B) = \rho(B, A) = 0. \tag{9}$$

It is straightforward to check that ρ is a potential function for the 2×2 game: any change in action by one player changes that player's payoff by the corresponding change in ρ. It follows from (7) that a potential function for the

[14] The concept of a potential game was introduced by Monderer and Shapley 1996. Note that the potential function is not unique: if $\rho^*(\mathbf{x})$ is a potential function then so is $\rho^*(\mathbf{x}) + a$ for any real constant a.

social interactions game (with $\lambda = 1$) is the sum of agents' private payoffs plus $(a - c)$ times the weighted sum of pairs coordinated on AA plus $(b - d)$ times the weighted sum of pairs coordinated on BB.

Consider for example the network game depicted in Figure 3.1. Each pair of interacting agents plays a coordination game in which the payoff to each agent is 1 if they coordinate on AA or BB, and 0 otherwise. Thus the potential of any given state equals the number of edges coordinated on AA, plus the number coordinated on BB, plus the private payoffs summed over all agents. It can be verified that the regional norms equilibrium in the figure has potential 82: namely, 54 from the coordinated edges plus 28 from the sum of the private payoffs. Moreover, this is the equilibrium with greatest potential. In particular, the global norm all-A has potential 80 and the global norm all-B has potential 76.

The existence of a potential function is very useful for determining the stochastically stable states, as the following result shows.

Proposition 3.1[15] *Suppose that the social interactions game has a potential function $\rho^*(\boldsymbol{x})$. Consider a dynamic process in which one player is chosen at random each period, and she revises her action according to a logit response function as in (3). Irrespective of the initial conditions, the long-run probability of each state $\boldsymbol{x}$ is*

$$\mu(\boldsymbol{x}) = e^{\beta\rho^*(\boldsymbol{x})} \Big/ \sum_{\boldsymbol{x}' \in X} e^{\beta\rho^*(\boldsymbol{x}')}. \tag{10}$$

When β is sufficiently large, the potential-maximizing states have probability close to one, that is, they are stochastically stable.

There is a connection between the potential of the coordination equilibria in a symmetric 2×2 coordination game and the concept of risk dominance. In the game described in (8), the potential of equilibrium AA equals $a - c$, which is the loss in payoff for a player that deviates to B. Similarly, the potential of equilibrium BB equals $b - d$, which is the loss in payoff for a player that deviates to A. AA is said to be *risk-dominant* if it is more costly to deviate from AA to BB than the other way around, that is, if $a - c > b - d$. Similarly, BB is risk-dominant if $a - c < b - d$. Thus *the risk-dominant equilibrium maximizes the potential function* of the 2×2 game. If the players are embedded in a social network and their private utilities equal 0, the potential of the social

[15] This result is due to Blume 1993.

interactions game is maximized when everyone plays the risk-dominant equilibrium. Proposition 3.1 shows that this is the stochastically stable equilibrium under the logit updating process. The next chapter discusses experiments with laboratory subjects that lend support to this model of the updating process.

3.7 Norms of cooperation

A classic example of a situation where the risk-dominant equilibrium may differ from the payoff-dominant equilibrium is Rousseau's Stag Hunt game.[16] Two hunters can cooperate to kill a stag but only if both forgo the chance to hunt easier game such as hares. Suppose that b is the benefit to each hunter from killing the stag, and c is the up-front cost of participating in the stag hunt, where $0 < c < b$. The payoff from hunting hares equals 0. The net payoffs from cooperating (C) or defecting (D) are as follows

	C	D
C	$b - c, b - c$	$-c, 0$
D	$0, -c$	$0, 0$

This is a potential game, and the cooperative equilibrium has potential $b - c$ whereas the defect equilibrium has potential c. Hence in a population of players with logit updating, the all-defect equilibrium will be the single most likely outcome in the long run unless $b \geq 2c$, that is, unless the individual benefit of cooperating is at least *twice* the cost.

This is a fairly demanding condition. Moreover the problem of incentivizing cooperation in the long run becomes even more acute when more players are involved. Suppose that m people can participate in a collective activity, such as a community fundraiser, a neighborhood clean-up campaign, the management of a common water resource, or the defense of common territory. The benefits accrue to all members of the community whether they participate or not. Let $x_i \geq 0$ be i's contribution (in time, effort, or money), and let $c_i(x_i)$ be the associated cost (loss of utility). Assume that $c_i(x_i)$ is increasing in x_i and $c_i(0) = 0$. Given the contributions $\boldsymbol{x} = (x_1, \ldots, x_n)$, let $b(\boldsymbol{x})$ be the benefit to

[16] There is an extensive literature on norms of cooperation that I shall not attempt to survey here. The purpose of this section is to show how the evolutionary framework can provide useful insights into the stability of cooperation in a population games setting.

each individual, which we shall assume is nondecreasing in each component x_i with $b(\mathbf{0}) = 0$. Thus the payoff to individual i is

$$U_i(\boldsymbol{x}) = b(\boldsymbol{x}) - c_i(x_i). \tag{11}$$

This m-person game has the potential function

$$\rho(\boldsymbol{x}) = b(\boldsymbol{x}) - \sum_j c_j(x_j). \tag{12}$$

Suppose that $\boldsymbol{x} = \mathbf{0}$ is a strict Nash equilibrium, that is, no single individual is motivated to contribute when no one else does. By assumption, the potential of this state is zero, hence under logit updating, complete non-cooperation will be the single most likely outcome in the long run unless there is some nonzero state $\boldsymbol{x}'$ such that

$$b(\boldsymbol{x}') \geq \sum_j c_j(x'_j). \tag{13}$$

In other words, *for some level of cooperation to be viable, there must exist a positive level of contributions such that each individual's benefit is at least as great as the total cost incurred by all contributors.*[17]

This result shows that the benefits from collective action may have to be very large (perhaps unrealistically large) relative to costs in order that some amount of cooperation be viable in the long run. Note, however, that this result only holds if there are no social costs imposed on non-cooperators. In practice, cooperators may punish non-cooperators by refusing to cooperate with them in the future, excluding them from group activities, or perhaps causing them physical harm. The problem with these enforcement mechanisms is that they are costly to execute and lead to higher-order problems of collective action, namely, how to coordinate on and enforce the punishments themselves.

A less costly method for maintaining cooperation is to increase the effective cost of defection by showing disapproval, disrespect, or withdrawing esteem from people who fail to cooperate. This mechanism is especially effective in small close-knit communities, such as professional associations, private clubs, volunteer organizations, and the small-scale hunting and foraging societies studied by anthropologists.[18] Moreover, expressions of disapproval (at

[17] Myatt and Wallace 2008 derive an analogous result for threshold team production games.

[18] The effectiveness of different mechanisms for supporting cooperation in small-scale societies is discussed by Bowles et al. 2012, Guala 2012, Mathew and Boyd 2014, Mathew 2017, and Boyd and Richerson 2022.

no monetary cost to the disapprover or the disapproved) have been shown to be effective at maintaining cooperation in laboratory settings.[19] These types of social penalties can be built into the players' payoff functions in much the same way as in the tipping game: those who contribute little or nothing relative to others suffer social stigma without any specific retribution being undertaken (for further examples see Chapter 7). The resulting social interactions game can greatly enhance the viability of cooperation. Although it may not be a potential game, its long-run dynamical behavior can still be characterized using the methods discussed earlier in this chapter.

[19] Masclet et al. 2003.

4

Norm Dynamics: Experiments

with Heinrich Nax

4.1 Experiments on Stag Hunt games

A basic premise of the framework discussed in the preceding chapters is that subjects learn over time, adjusting their behavior in light of what other subjects are doing, but with some idiosyncratic variation in their behavior. Experiments with laboratory subjects support this premise: they usually play some form of best reply to their perception of the current state (or fairly recent states), although they occasionally deviate. Most experiments show that the deviation probability tends to decrease the greater the prospective loss in utility, and that in these cases the logit model fits the data reasonably well.[1] This chapter discusses some of these results and how they relate to the dynamic models of equilibrium selection treated in the preceding chapter.

A large number of experiments focus on symmetric 2×2 coordination games in which the risk-dominant equilibrium differs from the payoff-dominant equilibrium (Stag Hunt games). The theory developed in Chapter 3 predicts that, over many repetitions of this type of game, the risk-dominant equilibrium will tend to be favored over the long run as the process shifts back and forth between the two equilibria. In practice, however, experiments are not run for nearly long enough to establish the long-run frequency of different equilibria, hence they do not actually constitute a test of this prediction. Nevertheless, the risk-dominant action does tend to be played more often than the payoff-dominant action when the two differ, especially when participants are matched and re-matched anonymously so there is no opportunity to build a reputation over repeated plays.[2] This apparent bias in favor of the risk-dominant equilibrium is driven in part by the fact that, in many of the

[1] See among others Battalio, Samuelson, and Van Huyck 2001, Mäs and Nax 2016, and Bilancini, Boncinelli, and Nax 2021.

[2] When subjects are allowed to communicate with one another, payoff-dominant equilibria are implemented more frequently than in fully anonymous settings (Clark and Sefton 2001, Clark et al. 2001).

The Dynamics of Social Norms. H. Peyton Young with Heinrich Nax, Oxford University Press.
 DOI: 10.1093/oso/9780198959052.003.0004

experiments, the payoffs are defined in such a way that the basin of attraction of the risk-dominant equilibrium is considerably larger than the basin of the payoff-dominant equilibrium. This enhances the probability that the initial state lies in the former rather than the latter, in which case the adjustment dynamics will continue to favor the risk-dominant equilibrium. Thus, although most experiments do not amount to a test of stochastic stability theory, they are useful in analyzing the nature of the dynamics, and they do tend to support the hypothesis that subjects' behavior can be represented, to a good approximation, as a 'noisy' best-response process. In what follows I shall discuss several experiments that are representative of this literature.

Battalio, Samuelson, and Van Huyck (2001) conducted a detailed study of three Stag Hunt games with different payoff configurations. In particular, they varied the *optimization premium*, that is, the payoff loss sustained by deviating from the payoff-dominant equilibrium, while holding fixed the relative size of the basins of attraction of the two equilibria. In each case, the risk-dominant basin was four times the size of the payoff-dominant basin. Their hypothesis was that the larger the optimization premium, the more attention subjects paid to choosing best responses, and the less noisy their responses were.

Each treatment involved eight subjects who were matched anonymously and played the game for 75 periods. The authors estimated the probability of deviating from best reply (given the subjects' choices in previous rounds) as a function of the payoff losses resulting from these deviations. They found that subjects' behavior, pooled over all subjects, was well-approximated by logit response functions, where the estimated response parameter β varied among treatments. Moreover, as hypothesized, the larger the optimization premium, the larger the estimated value of β, and the less likely subjects were to deviate from best response. Here I shall focus on subjects' period-by-period behavior to illustrate how the adjustment dynamics look in actual practice.

The game payoff matrices and their associated dynamics are shown in Figure 4.1. The state at each point in time represents the proportion of times that the payoff-dominant action was played over the preceding five periods, thus smoothing out some of the period-by-period variability that occurred between periods. The boundary between the two basins of attraction (the *separatrix)* is indicated by the horizontal line at 80%. Given an initial state below this line, the unperturbed best-response dynamics stays below it and converges to the risk-dominant equilibrium with probability one. In the presence of perturbations, the process can jump over the separatrix and into the basin of attraction of the payoff-dominant equilibrium; moreover, this actually occurred in some of the experiments, as Figure 4.1 demonstrates. For example, in the top treatment, there were two instances where the process

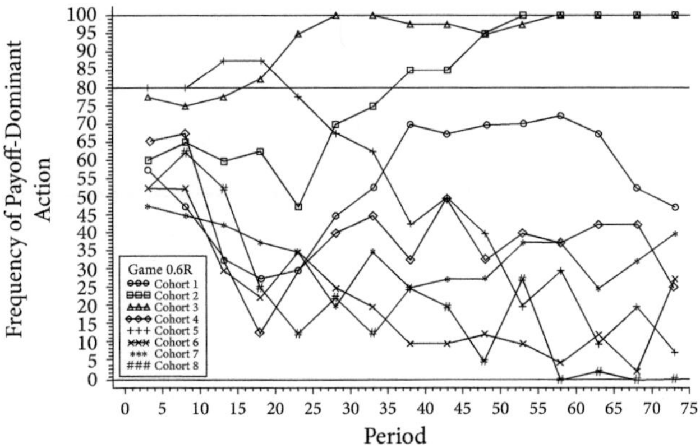

45,45	0,42
42,0	12,12

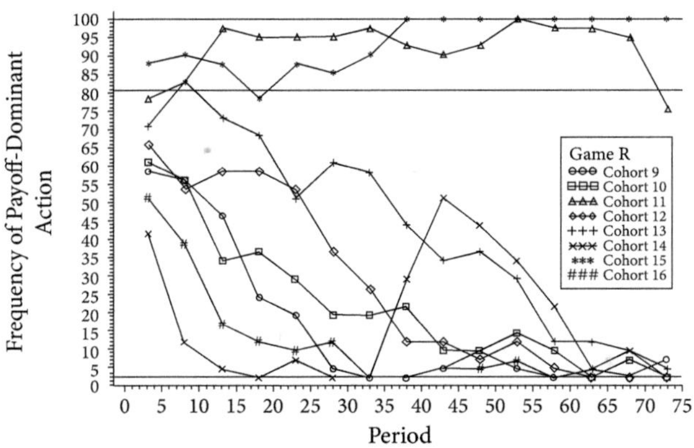

45,45	0,40
40,0	20,20

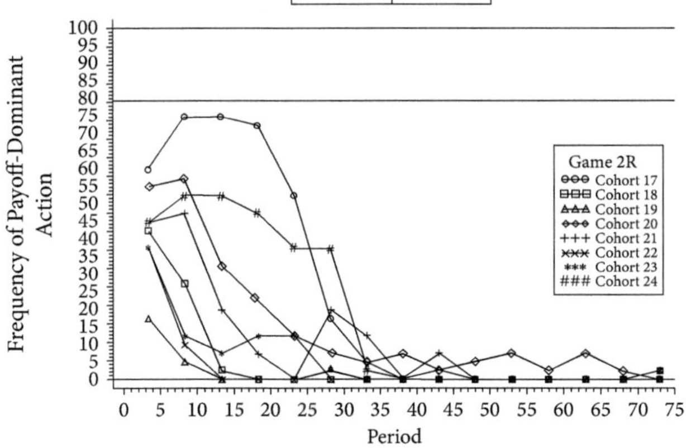

45,45	0,35
35,0	40,40

Figure 4.1 Dynamic learning behavior in three Stag Hunt games. The vertical axis gives the mean frequency of the payoff-dominant action over successive five-period intervals. The payoff matrix is shown below each graph.

Source: Figure 6 in Battalio, R., Samuelson, L., and Van Huyck, J. 2001. "Optimization incentives and coordination failure in laboratory Stag Hunt games." *Econometrica* 69: 749–764.

began below the horizontal line (i.e., in the risk-dominant basin), and after several periods moved above it and stayed there, eventually coming close to the payoff-dominant equilibrium. In another instance, the initial state was on the separatrix itself, and from there the process moved briefly into the payoff-dominant basin, but then fell out again and converged to the risk-dominant equilibrium. In the middle treatment, there is an instance where the initial state was below the separatrix and the process subsequently moved above it, but near the end of the session the process reverted to the risk-dominant basin. In the bottom treatment the initial state was always in the risk-dominant basin and the process moved quite rapidly to nearly everyone playing the risk-dominant action.

These results are consistent with the dynamic behavior one would expect in a best-response model with stochastic perturbations. It should be noted, however, that this behavior is aggregated over many individuals. As we shall see in the next few sections, other experiments show that, even though overall the dynamic process can be well approximated by a perturbed best-response model such as logit, the learning behavior of *individual* subjects is quite varied and complex.

4.2 Experiments on network games

Learning dynamics have also been studied experimentally for games in which players are located at the vertices of a network and they interact only with their immediate neighbors. Here I discuss two investigations of subjects' adjustment behavior and their implications for equilibrium selection (Mäs and Nax 2016, Bilancini, Boncinelli, and Nax 2021). In both studies the network has a ring structure, much like one of the treatments in the Name Game discussed in Chapter 2. Unlike that game, where the choice of action was open-ended, here subjects can choose just one of two colors: white (w) or gray (g). Subjects are endowed with heterogeneous preferences: "White" subjects favor color w whereas "Gray" subjects favor color g (see Figure 4.2). They are located around the ring in alternating sequence and each is linked with the nearest two agents on either side (the network is regular of degree 4).

Payoffs. Agents receive a payoff of 1 for each neighbor with whom they coordinate, and 0 otherwise. In addition, an agent receives a bonus of P for playing his favorite color. Two cases are considered: P = 1 and P = 3. This set-up defines a potential game, where the *potential of a state equals the total number of coordinated edges plus P times the number of agents playing their favorite color.*

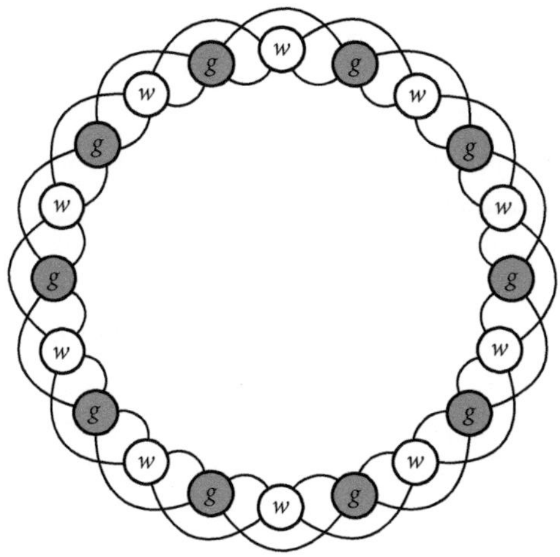

Figure 4.2 A ring network with 20 agents and two types in alternating sequence.

Source: Figure 1 in Bilancini, E., Boncinelli, L., and Nax, H. H. 2021. "What noise matters? Experimental evidence for stochastic deviations in social norms." *Journal of Behavioral and Experimental Economics* 90(4): 101626.

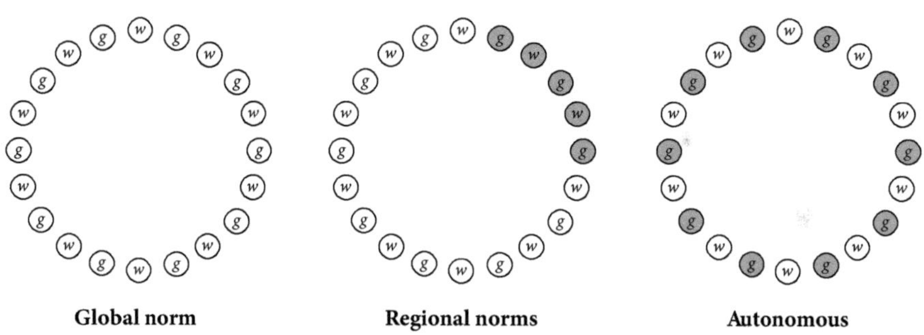

Figure 4.3 Three types of equilibria when the favorite-color payoff is P = 1.

Equilibria. When P = 1, there are three types of equilibria, as shown in Figure 4.3. There are two global norms (white and gray), one autonomous equilibrium, and many segmented equilibria (regional norms). In the latter, each segment consists of five or more consecutive agents choosing the same color, where the players at the end of each segment choose their favorite color. When P = 3, the autonomous and global configurations are equilibria but not the regional arrangements. Note that the global and segmented equilibria illustrate the phenomenon of *compression*: individual heterogeneity in preferences is masked by the incentive to coordinate with one's neighbors. In what follows I shall focus on the case where P = 1.

At the start of a given session, twenty subjects were assigned a type (White or Gray) and a position on the network. They were informed of their own type but not of their position in the network or the types of their neighbors. They were also provided with a payoff table showing their payoffs as a function of the number of their (anonymous) neighbors choosing each action. At the end of each period every player learned the number of their neighbors who chose white or gray in that period, hence over time they knew the history of play by their neighbors (but not who played what). At the start of each period, one randomly drawn player was given the opportunity to revise his or her choice, hence revision opportunities were asynchronous. Three sessions were conducted for each value of P, each lasting for 150 rounds.

4.3 Analysis of the learning dynamics

A useful starting point for analyzing the dynamics is to examine the frequency of deviations from myopic best reply given the choices of one's neighbors in the prior round. The results, pooled over all subjects and all sessions with $P = 1$, are shown in Table 4.1. Column (1) shows the payoff from choosing one's favorite color, conditional on the proportion x of one's neighbors choosing that same color; column (2) shows the payoff from playing the opposite of one's favorite color conditional on x; while column (1–2) shows the payoff difference $(-3 + 8x)$ between (1) and (2). Notice that the probability of choosing one's favorite color increases quite rapidly as a function of this difference, as can be seen from column (y).

The data in Table 4.1 represent average behavior at the level of the group, not the behavior of specific individuals. A detailed look at subjects' period-by-period choices reveals that there is significant variation in their probability of deviating from myopic best reply; moreover their behavior in the current period can depend in a complex way on the pattern of their realized payoffs in prior periods.

One natural question, for example, is whether a given subject's behavior depends only on the *most recent* choice of actions by her neighbors, or depends as well on their choices in earlier periods. Mäs and Nax (2016) show that, although subjects sometimes did look more than one period back, look-backs of more than five periods were rare. Moreover, the inclusion of these periods in the behavioral model did little to improve its predictive power: subjects that

Table 4.1 (1) is the payoff from choosing one's favorite color given the proportion (x) of one's neighbors who are choosing that color, whereas (2) is the payoff from choosing the other color; (1–2) is the payoff difference between (1) and (2); (y) is the probability of playing one's favorite color conditional on x; (s.d.) is the binomial standard deviation of y. Data were aggregated over all sessions with P = 1.

Who plays my color?	(x)	(1)	(2)	(1–2)	#	(y)	s.d.
Nobody	0/4	1	4	−3	3631	0.0377	0.0032
Only one other	1/4	2	3	−1	650	0.2923	0.0178
Half of the other	2/4	3	2	1	443	0.9165	0.0131
Most of the other	3/4	4	1	3	520	0.9904	0.0043
Everyone	4/4	5	0	5	3696	0.9992	0.0005

Source: Bilancini, E., Boncinelli, L., and Nax, H. H. "What noise matters? Experimental evidence for stochastic deviations in social norms." *Journal of Behavioral and Experimental Economics* 90(4): 101626.

made a myopic best response would have made the same choice with high probability if they looked back several periods and chose a best response to the average of their neighbors' behavior in those periods.

Another finding was that a subject's probability of deviating from myopic best response depended on both the *level* and *pattern* of her recent payoffs. A relatively low payoff in the prior period triggered a deviation more often than when the subject's payoff was relatively high. Similarly, a deviation was triggered more often if the subject experienced a payoff *decrease* in the prior period compared to her payoff two periods earlier. This *asymmetric search behavior* is a key feature of various learning rules, such as trial-and-error learning (Young 2009).

A further finding was *favorite-color bias*: subjects tended to choose their favorite color more often than would be warranted solely from its extra payoff. In particular, some subjects played their favorite color repeatedly in spite of suffering payoff losses from doing so. Apparently, they believed that by being stubborn they could eventually induce their neighbors to switch (which usually turned out not to work).

To gain a better sense of the variation in subjects' period-by-period behavior, consider the path of play shown in Figure 4.4. In this case 20 agents, favoring either red or blue, were placed in alternating sequence around a ring (analogously to Figure 4.2), and the bonus from choosing one's favorite color was P = 1. Squares represent best replies to the previous period's distribution,

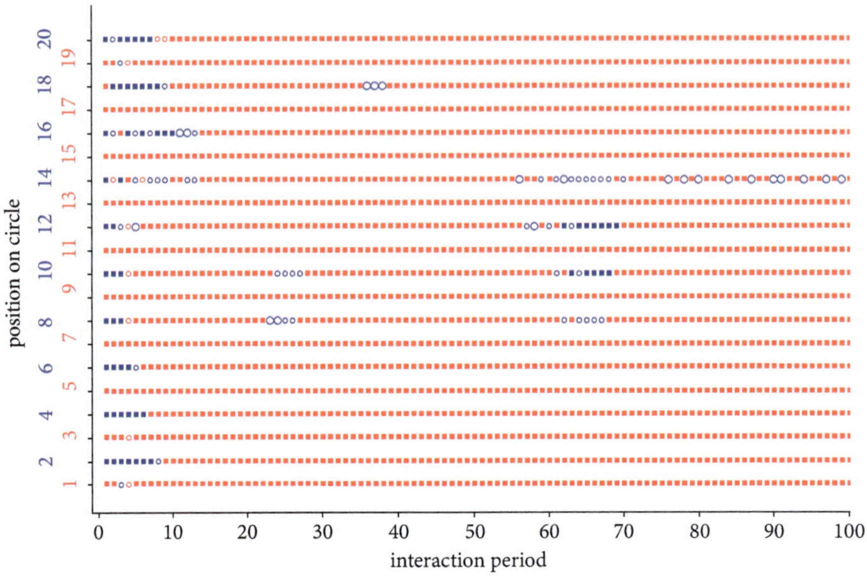

Figure 4.4 Typical pattern of play when P = 1. Solid entries correspond to best replies, small hollow entries to non-best replies with low deviation cost, large hollow entries to non-best replies with high deviation costs.
Source: Laboratory experiments conducted by H. H. Nax.

that is, to the choices of the agent's four neighbors in the previous round. Small hollow entries represent non-best replies with a deviation cost equal to 1; large hollow entries represent non-best replies with a deviation cost greater than 1. In this session, all but one subject began by playing his or her favorite color. However, the process did not revert to the autonomous equilibrium. Instead, a red segment began to form and grew quite rapidly until by period 12 a global red equilibrium had been reached. Nevertheless, convergence was only temporary: throughout the session a few Blue individuals reverted to choosing blue repeatedly even though this strategy failed to induce their neighbors to change.

4.4 Stochastic stability and equilibrium fragility

One aim of the experiments by Bilancini et al. was to examine which equilibria are most likely to emerge over the course of play, and whether they correspond to the predictions of stochastic stability theory. As noted in the discussion of Stag Hunt games, experiments are not conducted for nearly enough periods to estimate the long-run probability of different states with much reliability. The problem is especially acute when the number of states is very large. In the preceding examples, there are 20 individuals, each of whom can choose between two colors. Suppose that each player conditions his choice on the actions of the others in the immediately preceding period. Then the relevant state space has cardinality 2^{20}, which is more than one million. If we suppose that players condition their choices on actions taken over several prior periods, the state space is vastly larger.

Instead of trying to estimate the long-run probability of each state, we can examine the relative "fragility" of a given equilibrium by computing the minimum number of deviations from best response that are needed to transit to some other equilibrium. For example, only one deviation is required to transit from the autonomous equilibrium to a segmented equilibrium consisting of regional norms (see Figure 4.3). Namely, suppose that a Gray agent deviates by playing white. If the next two agents to revise are her two Gray neighbors, their best response is also to choose white. Hence after three steps and one deviation the process has transited to a segmented equilibrium. Similarly, it may be verified that it takes only one deviation to transit from a segmented equilibrium to a nearby segmented equilibrium (or to a global equilibrium). However, it requires at least three deviations to move from a global equilibrium to some other equilibrium. In this sense the global equilibria are the least "fragile" of the various equilibria. Although it turns out that, in this example, the least fragile equilibria are also stochastically stable (the most likely in the long run), in general this need not be the case.

Counting the number of deviations to transit between equilibria is only appropriate when all deviations have the same probability. In the experiments of Bilancini et al. this is decidedly not the case: as inspection of Table 4.1 shows, the probability of a non-best response decreases as the prospective loss in payoff increases. In fact, the response function is well-approximated by a logit model. To see this, let R(X) be the probability of choosing one's favorite color divided by the probability of choosing the other color, as a function of the payoff difference X between the two choices. Figure 4.5 shows that Y = log R(X) is very nearly linear in X with slope 1.31 and intercept 0.69. This translates into the logit response function $f(x) = 1/(1 + e^{-1.31(.527-3+8x)})$ shown in Figure 4.6 where $f(x)$ is the probability of choosing one's favorite color when x is the proportion of one's neighbors choosing that color. Since the nominal payoff advantage to choosing one's favorite color is $-3 + 8x$, the constant .527 represents an additional payoff reflecting the favorite-color bias mentioned earlier.

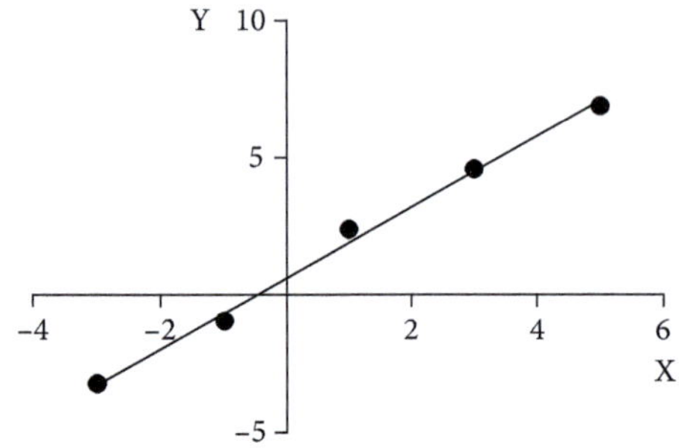

Figure 4.5 Log odds (Y) of choosing one's favorite color as a function of the difference in payoff (X) between choosing one's favorite color versus the opposite color. Slope = 1.31 (0.05), intercept = 0.69. $R^2 = 0.995$.

Source: Based on data in Table 4.1.

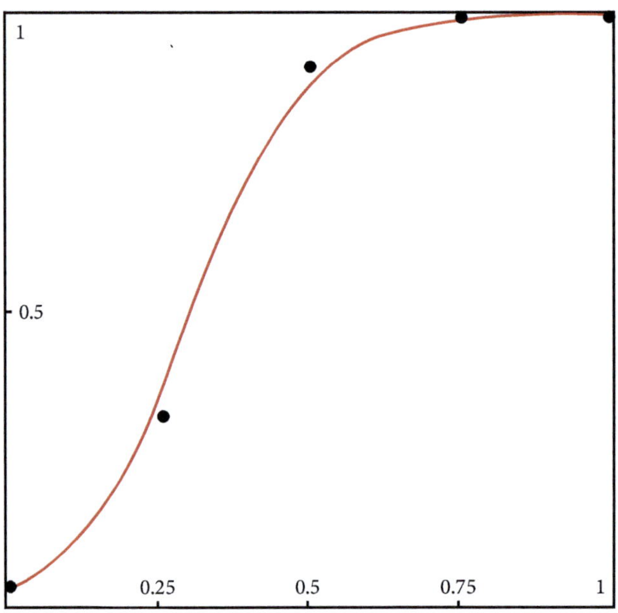

$f(x) = 1/\ (1+e^{-1.31(.527-3+8x)})$

Figure 4.6 Probability of choosing one's favorite color when x is the proportion of one's neighbors playing that color.

Table 4.2 Effective potential ρ^* of the three types of equilibria when P = 1.

Autonomous	$1.527 \times 20 + 20 = 50.540$
Regional	$1.527 \times 11 + 34 = 50.797$
Global	$1.527 \times 10 + 40 = 55.270$

We can compute the long-run probability of each state by exploiting the fact that the underlying game is a potential game. The favorite-color bias can be incorporated directly into the potential function by defining the *effective potential* of state $\boldsymbol{x}$ to be

$$\rho^*(\boldsymbol{x}) = 1.527\left(\#\ \textit{agents playing favorite color}\right) + \#\ \textit{adjacent pairs coordinated on the same color.}$$

Table 4.2 shows the effective potential of the three types of equilibria. It follows from Proposition 3.1 that the long-run probability of each state $\boldsymbol{x}$ is proportional to $e^{1.31\rho^*(x)}$, and hence the probability of $\boldsymbol{x}$ is $e^{1.31\rho^*(x)} / \sum_y e^{1.31\rho^*(y)}$.

Given the very large number of states and the high level of noise, the model predicts that none of the equilibrium states will be particularly probable in an absolute sense. Of greater interest is their *relative* probability. From Table 4.2 we can deduce, for example, that each of the two global equilibria is $e^{1.31(55.270 - 50.540)} = 491$ times more likely than the autonomous equilibrium. Of course, this estimate only holds if the deviation probabilities remain constant over many periods. In fact, Mäs and Nax (2016) and Bilancini et al. (2021) found that the deviation probabilities tended to decrease over the course of the experiment (β increased), in which case the frequency difference between the global and autonomous equilibria would be even greater.

4.5 Challenges to testing the theory

The experiments discussed above are broadly consistent with the predictions of a perturbed best-response model, but as previously noted, they do not amount to an empirical test of stochastic stability theory for several reasons. First, stochastic stability is concerned with the most likely state to be observed *over the long run*. To test its validity, one would need to run enough repetitions of the game to observe the frequency of switching between equilibria, not just the likelihood of transiting to an equilibrium for the first time, which is heavily dependent on initial conditions. Experiments are not run for long enough to estimate these switching probabilities with any accuracy. It turns out, however, that the theory developed so far has much to say about the intermediate-run behavior of the evolutionary dynamics, and it can be applied even when deviations from best response are not very small. In this case transitions between equilibria can occur much more rapidly. Moreover, the rate of transition depends on the structure of the interactions between the agents (the network topology), as well as on the size and distribution of the stochastic perturbations. This is the subject of the next chapter.

5

Norm shifts, Tipping Points, and Transition Times

5.1 Tipping points

As the preceding chapters have shown, norm dynamics are complex and somewhat erratic. Established ways of doing things may gradually and almost imperceptibly become undermined by changes in behaviors and actions by a few individuals, then suddenly give way as a new norm displaces the old. The transition is not assured however: a novel way of doing things may gain ground at first, only to stall and then die out. Once enough people have adopted a new way of doing things, however, it becomes very likely that the process will "take off' and a new norm will emerge due to positive feedback effects. The threshold where take-off occurs is commonly known as the *tipping point*, a phenomenon first studied in detail by Thomas Schelling.

How exactly is the tipping point determined and how long does it take to reach it? This issue is of particular importance if the objective is to induce norm shifts by some form of intervention. It is also crucial to understanding how long it might take an undesirable norm to unravel on its own unless some type of intervention is undertaken. In this chapter I shall study tipping points in detail using the analytical framework laid out in Chapter 3.

The conventional definition of tipping point is the *minimum proportion* of adopters beyond which the new way of doing things becomes the best response for those who have not yet adopted. In a fully mixed population, where everyone interacts with everyone else and everyone chooses a best response given the current state, this threshold is straightforward to calculate from the game payoffs. However, when people interact only with their neighbors in a social network, and their responses are subject to random perturbations, a different concept of tipping point is called for.

This chapter is based on Kreindler and Young 2013, and on Arieli, Babichenko, Peretz, and Young 2020.

The Dynamics of Social Norms. H. Peyton Young, Oxford University Press.
 DOI: 10.1093/oso/9780198959052.003.0005

5.2 Nominal vs effective tipping points in fully mixed populations

To fix ideas, consider a large population of m individuals such that everyone interacts with everyone else with equal probability and everyone has the same preferences. Assume that the payoffs from each pairwise interaction are given by the following 2×2 coordination game:

$$\begin{array}{ccc} & A & B \\ A & \alpha, \alpha & 0, 0 \\ B & 0, 0 & 1, 1 \end{array} \quad \alpha > 1. \tag{1}$$

In this game the payoff-dominant and risk-dominant equilibria coincide, which simplifies the notation. A similar analysis holds for 2×2 coordination games where the risk-dominant equilibrium is not payoff-dominant. Let the *state* of the system at time t be the proportion x^t of the population who are currently playing A. The possible states are the fractions k/m where k is an integer between 0 and m. In state x^t, the expected payoff to playing A equals αx^t while the expected payoff to playing B equals $1 - x^t$.

Assume that in each period one agent is drawn at random and has the opportunity to update her choice. I shall assume that the length of time between any two successive updates is $1/m$, hence the number of updates over a given interval of time is proportional to the size of the population. Define the *response function* $f(x)$ to be the *probability* that an updating agent chooses A in period $t + 1$, given that $x = x^t$ is the state in period t. If agents invariably choose a strict best response given the current state, then $f(x) = 1$ whenever $x > \tau = 1/(1 + \alpha)$. This is the *nominal tipping point* from all-B to all-A.[1]

This is an idealized scenario: in reality there will be considerable variability in agents' behavior due to experimentation, misperceptions of the state, heterogeneity in their payoffs, and other idiosyncratic factors. As we have seen in prior chapters, experiments and field data are consistent with the proposition that deviations from best response occur with a probability that decreases the larger the expected payoff loss from the deviation. This is a property of the logit response function, but it also holds for many other perturbed best-response models, such as best response subject to normally distributed payoff shocks.

The stochastic nature of the process can have a significant impact on the *effective tipping point*, namely, the point at which the *expected* proportion of

[1] For expositional convenience I shall ignore the fact that x takes on only discrete values; when m is large this does not change the analysis in any significant way.

adopters increases and continues to do so until at least half the population is playing the new action. More formally, define the *effective tipping point* from all-B to all-A to be the least proportion τ^* such that $x < f(x)$ on the interval $\tau^* < x \leq 1/2$. Whenever $x < f(x)$ the probability that a revising agent chooses A is greater than the current proportion choosing A, hence next period the *expected* proportion of A-players increases. Once the effective tipping point is reached, the proportion of A-players increases in expectation until it constitutes a majority of the population. (Indeed, the proportion of A-players may continue to increase well beyond a majority depending on the shape of the response function.)

The effective tipping point can be considerably less than the nominal tipping point, as Figure 5.1 illustrates. The nominal tipping point occurs at the value of x where the expected payoff to A equals the expected payoff to B, that is, at $\tau = 0.40$. By contrast, the effective tipping point is the middle of the three crossing points, namely $\tau^* = 0.27$. Once the proportion of As exceeds τ^*, it increases in expectation until the process comes close to the third crossing point. This does not mean that the proportion of As advances monotonically over

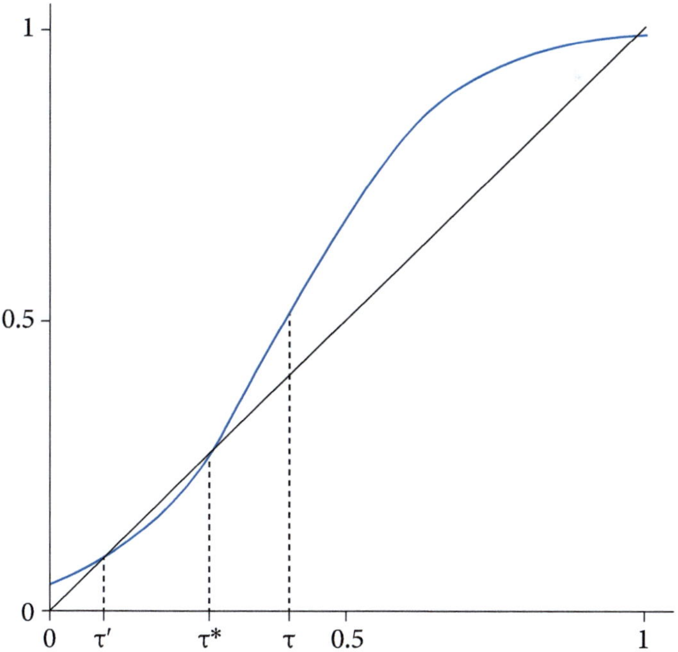

Figure 5.1 The logit response function for $\alpha = 1.5$ and $\beta = 3$. The nominal tipping point is $\tau = 0.40$ whereas the effective tipping point is $\tau^* = 0.27$.

this interval; the proportion could advance or decline quite erratically depending on the realization of the stochastic shocks. (This erratic behavior is evident in the behavior of individual agents in experimental settings, as we saw in Chapter 4.)

5.3 Transition times in fully mixed populations

The transition to a new equilibrium advances (in an expected sense) once the effective tipping point is reached, and it continues to advance until at least a majority of agents have adopted the new action. But how long does the process take to reach that point? Consider the example in Figure 5.1 and suppose that the process starts in the all-B state ($x = 0$). From there until the first crossing point (τ'), the response function lies above the diagonal, hence in this interval the proportion of As increases in expectation. The intuition is that, although the status quo action B is the best response throughout this interval, stochastic perturbations imply that the new action A is chosen some of the time, and the probability with which it is chosen exceeds its current proportion. Between τ' and τ^*, the response function lies *below* the diagonal, which implies that the expected proportion of As *decreases*. Once the process enters this interval, it becomes difficult to escape. In fact, it can be shown that the expected waiting time to escape a neighborhood of τ' and reach a majority of A-players grows exponentially large as the population size goes to infinity.

It turns out, however, that when the process is sufficiently "noisy" (due to random perturbations), the response function can lie above the diagonal over the whole interval [0, 1/2], as shown in Figure 5.2.

In this case, the effective tipping point equals zero, and the proportion of the population choosing the new action A increases in expectation right from the start. Moreover, the expected waiting time to reach a majority of A-players is bounded independently of the population size.[2]

To illustrate, suppose that the payoffs are as in (1), and consider the logit response function:

$$f(x) = \frac{e^{\beta \alpha x}}{e^{\beta a x} + e^{\beta(1-x)}} \textit{ for some } \beta > 0. \qquad (2)$$

[2] A similar analysis holds for any response curve that lies above the diagonal on the interval [0, 1/2], whether or not it is generated by a logit process.

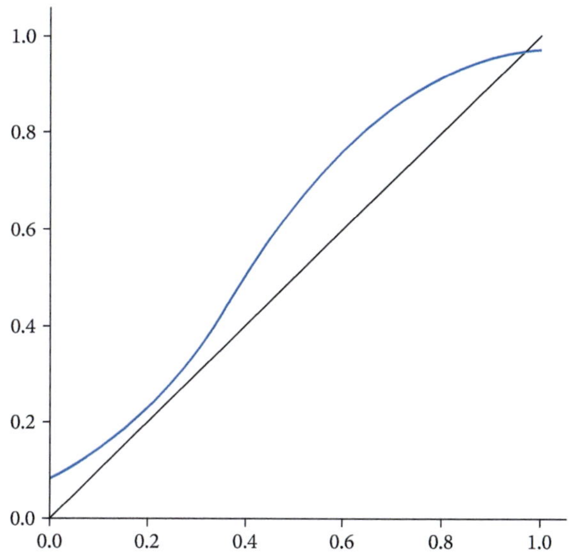

Figure 5.2 The logit response function for $\alpha = 1.5$ and $\beta = 2.4$. The function does not cross the diagonal anywhere below $x = .5$.

Given a population of m individuals, let $W(\alpha, \beta, m)$ denote the *expected waiting time* to reach a state where a *majority* of the population is playing A, starting from the state where everyone is playing B. (Recall our assumption that the number of revisions per unit of time is proportional to the population size m.) The transition from all-B to half-A is *fast* if $W(\alpha, \beta, m)$ is bounded above independently of m. It is *slow* if the expected waiting time grows without bound as m becomes arbitrarily large.

The boundary between fast and slow regimes is very sharp and is defined by the values of α and β for which the response function is tangent to the diagonal. To illustrate, it will be useful to make a change of variable. Let $\varepsilon = 1/(1 + e^{\beta})$ be the probability that an agent plays A in the all-B state. Figure 5.3 illustrates the boundary between the slow and fast transition regimes as a function of α and ε. Combinations of α and ε that lie just below the dashed line can take arbitrarily long (in expectation) to reach a given target above 1/2 as the population size grows, whereas combinations just above this line reach the target in a bounded number of time periods independently of the population size. The figure shows, moreover, that to reach a very high target (in this case 99% playing A) can take relatively few periods in expectation.

The expected waiting time changes dramatically for even minor differences in the payoffs and a given level of noise, as shown in Table 5.1.

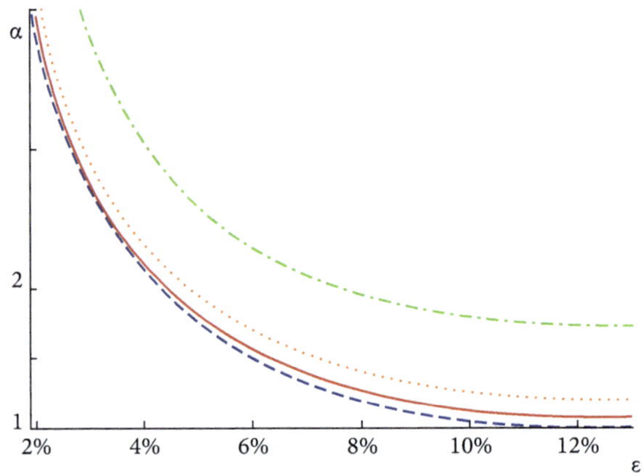

Figure 5.3 Expected number of periods, as a function of α and $\varepsilon = 1/(1 + e^{\beta})$, until at least 99% of the population is playing A, starting from the state where no one plays A. Forty periods (solid curve), 20 periods (dotted curve),10 periods (dash-dotted curve). Results obtained by Monte Carlo simulations.

Source: Figure 5 in Kreindler, G. E., Young, H. P. 2013, "Fast convergence in evolutionary equilibrium selection," *Games and Economic Behavior* 80: 39–67.

Table 5.1 Expected waiting times until at least 99% of the population chooses A, starting from the all-B state, for $\alpha = 1.7$, $\alpha = 1.8$, and $\varepsilon = .05$. Results obtained by Monte Carlo simulations.

	$m = 100$	$m = 1000$	$m = 10{,}000$	$m = \infty$
$\alpha = 1.7$	32.65	102.88	33,691.57	∞
$\alpha = 1.8$	24.44	33.59	35.29	35.19

Source: Table 1 in Kreindler and Young 2013, "Fast convergence in evolutionary equilibrium selection." *Games and Economic Behavior* 80: 39–67.

The next result shows that, when the process is sufficiently noisy (β is sufficiently small), the effective tipping point equals zero for all values $\alpha > 1$. In other words, there is a level of noise above which the transition from all-B to half-A is *always fast.*

Theorem 5.1[3] *Given the payoffs in (1) and a logit response process with response parameter β, the effective tipping point equals zero if*

$$0 < \beta \leq 2 \quad \text{or } \beta > 2 \text{ and } \alpha > (e^{\beta-1} + 4 - e)/\beta - 1. \tag{3}$$

[3] This result follows from Kreindler and Young 2013, Theorem 1, with a change of notation.

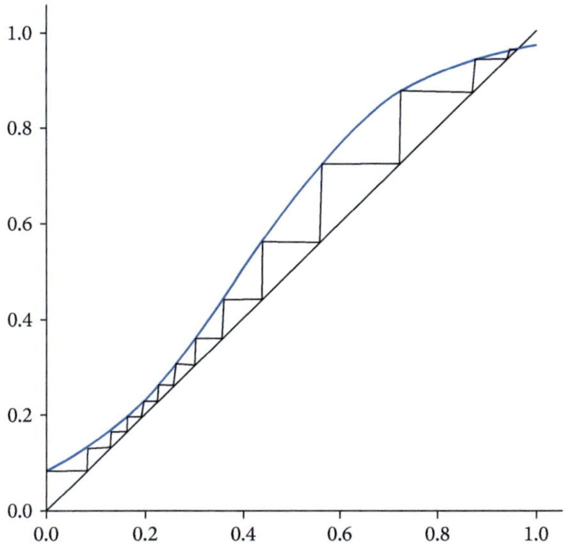

Figure 5.4 Stepwise adjustment dynamics for the response function in Figure 5.2.

The dynamics are illustrated informally in Figure 5.4. Starting from the all-B state $x_0 = 0$, imagine that the process jumps to the state $x_1 = f(x_0)$, then to the state $x_2 = f(x_1)$, and so forth. (This is purely conceptual; in reality the behavior is stochastic.) The proportion of As advances at a decreasing rate until it squeezes through the bottleneck, after which the proportion of As advances at an increasing rate until it slows down as the upper crossing point is approached.

The preceding results are framed in terms of a coordination game in which the payoff-dominant equilibrium coincides with the risk-dominant equilibrium. If the two differ, as in Stag Hunt games, then analogous results apply to transitions from the payoff-dominant equilibrium to the risk-dominant one. In this case the latter is stochastically stable and the transition is fast if the noise is sufficiently large (β is sufficiently small).

A similar analysis can be carried out for the tipping game (see Chapter 3, expression (2)), where it is assumed that the payoffs satisfy g < 2 < s. When g + s > 4, the H-norm is risk-dominant but not payoff-dominant. It follows from Theorem 5.1 that, under the logit response function, the process will transition from the L-norm to the H-norm quite rapidly when the response parameter is sufficiently small. In particular, by letting $\alpha = (s - 2) / (2 - g)$ and $\varepsilon = 1/(1 + e^{\beta(2-g)})$ we can use Figure 5.3 to estimate the expected number of periods until at least 99% of the population is playing H for different combinations of α and ε. These results show that transitions between norms can occur surprisingly quickly even in very large populations.

5.4 Transition times in networks

In this section I turn to the more general situation where agents are situated in a social network and they respond only to the choices of their neighbors. I allow for the possibility that agents exert different degrees of influence on their neighbors, and the direction of influence may be *asymmetric*: agent *i* may influence *j*'s choice more strongly than *j* influences *i*'s choice. I shall also allow for general response functions (not only logit) that could arise from payoff shocks, misperceptions of what the neighbors are doing, or just plain mistakes. The details of the interaction structure can have a significant impact on the effective tipping point as well as on the speed with which a norm transition occurs. Nevertheless, one can obtain very general results on the expected rate of transition when the response function $f(x)$ lies strictly above the diagonal on some interval $0 \leq x \leq q$, as in the preceding analysis.

Given a population of m agents, an *interaction structure* is an m x m matrix $\mathbf{P} = (p_{ij})$ whose entries are non-negative and every row sums to 1. The value p_{ij} is the *relative influence* that *j* exerts on *i*. *The state at time t* is an m-vector z^t such that

$$\begin{aligned} z_i^t &= 1 \text{ if agent } i \text{ plays } A \text{ at } t \\ z_i^t &= 0 \text{ if agent } i \text{ plays } B \text{ at } t. \end{aligned} \tag{4}$$

Assume that each agent updates once per period in expectation, and that their updating opportunities are independently distributed. Assume further that if a given agent *i* receives such an opportunity in period *t*, she chooses action A with probability $f(x_i^t)$, where

$$x_i^t = \sum_j p_{ij} z_j^t. \tag{5}$$

In other words, *i* reacts via the *response function* $f(x_i^t)$ to the summary statistic x_i^t of the actions taken by the other players, weighted by their relative influence on *i*. The example in Figure 5.5 illustrates the connection between x_i and the choices of *i*'s neighbors, as represented by the indicator variables $z_j = 0$ or 1 (the time superscripts are omitted).

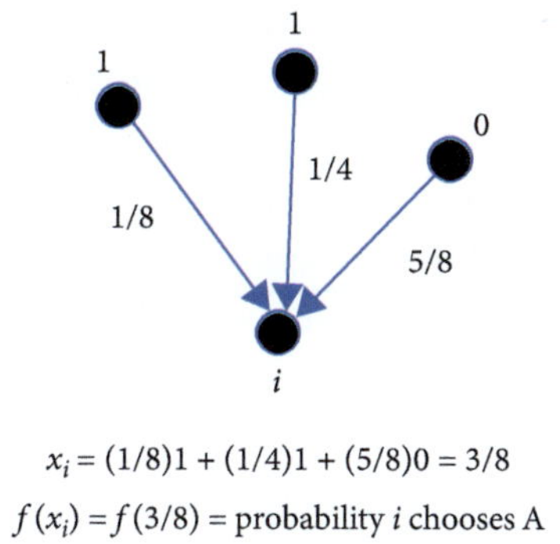

Figure 5.5 Illustration of the relationship between the variables z_j and the variable x_i when individual i has three neighbors.

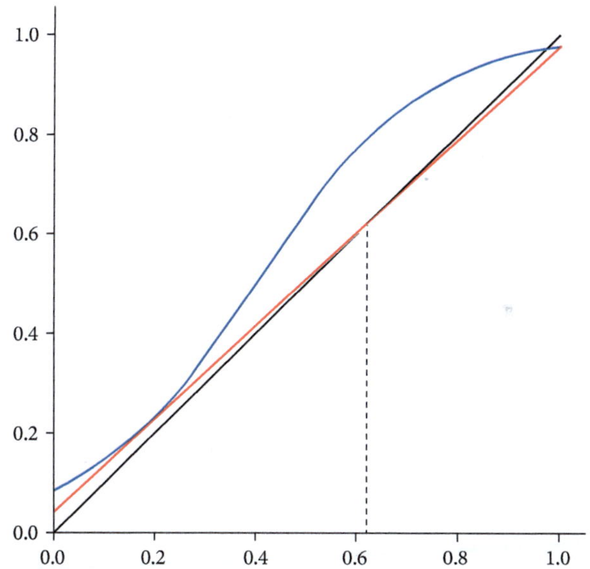

Figure 5.6 The lower envelope (red line) of the response function in Figure 5.2.

Given a response function $f(x)$, let $\tilde{f}(x)$ be the straight line with minimum slope that lies below $f(x)$ and satisfies $\tilde{f}(1) = f(1)$. This is the *lower envelope of* $f(x)$ as illustrated in Figure 5.6.

Let $p = p(\tilde{f})$ be the unique crossing point of $\tilde{f}$ and the 45-degree line, that is, the fixed point of the function $\tilde{f}$:

$$p = \tilde{f}(0)/[1 - (\tilde{f}(1) - \tilde{f}(0))]. \quad (6)$$

In Figure 5.6 the fixed point is $p = 0.616$, where the dashed line intersects the x-axis. The point where the response function intersects the y-axis is $\tilde{f}(0) = 0.043$.

The analysis of waiting times in Section 5.3 shows that a sufficient condition for fast transition from all-B to a target proportion q of A-players is that the response function should lie strictly above the diagonal on the interval $[0, q]$. In the present, more general setting, it turns out that sufficient conditions for fast transition are that: i) the lower envelope have a positive y-intercept ($\tilde{f}(0) > 0$), and ii) the target q is less than the fixed point of $\tilde{f}$.

Theorem 5.2[4] *Suppose the lower envelope of the response function has fixed point p and satisfies $\tilde{f}(0) > 0$. For any target level of adoption q satisfying $0 < q < p$, and any interaction structure P, the expected waiting time until the first time that q or more of the agents are playing A is at most*

$$(7.2/\tilde{f}(0))[1 + \ln(p/(p - q))]. \tag{7}$$

This result provides a uniform upper bound on the expected waiting time until the stochastic process first reaches a given level of adoption $q < p$, where *the bound holds for all interaction structures of any size and topological complexity.*

For specific classes of networks, the expected waiting times can be much shorter. For example, in the network games discussed in Chapter 4, it takes at most a handful of deviants (in some cases only one deviant) to tip the process from one equilibrium into the basin of attraction of another. Given the observed probability with which subjects deviate in experimental settings, the expected waiting time to transit between equilibria can be quite short—certainly much less than the bound in (7).

The expected waiting time can also be much lower in regular networks. Suppose that all agents have the same number of neighbors and all influence weights are equal. It can be shown that, in this case, the expected waiting time to transit from all-B to a proportion q of A-players is bounded above by $1 + (p/\tilde{f}(0))\ln(p/(p - q))$ for all sufficiently large populations.[5] This is substantially less than the bound in (7); moreover, it is often quite small. In Figure 5.6, for example, the fixed point is $p = 0.616$ and the y-intercept is $\tilde{f}(0) = 0.043$. If the target proportion is $q = 0.5$, then in a large, globally mixed population the expected waiting time would be at most 25 periods.

[4] Arieli, Babichenko, Peretz, and Young 2020, Theorem 3.1.
[5] This follows from Arieli, Babichenko, Peretz, and Young 2020, Proposition 6.1.

It should be emphasized that these are theoretical upper bounds, and the actual behavior of subjects in experimental settings could depart substantially from these estimates.[6] The theoretical results do suggest, however, that the expected waiting time to observe a norm shift—as expressed by the number of revisions per individual—can be surprisingly short even in large populations. It also bears emphasizing that the actual speed of norm shifts (as measured in real time) depends crucially on the rate at which individuals update their choices. If I am deciding how to dress when going to the office, I make a new decision every business day. If I am a landlord deciding how much to offer the tenant on my farm, I would only update once a year. If I am a parent deciding whether to circumcise my daughter, I would make a decision only once for each daughter. In the first case a norm transition might occur in a matter of weeks or months, whereas in the latter case it could take many years.

5.5 Tipping points, contagion, and network structure

In this section, I shall examine the question of which agents are best-placed to *induce* a norm shift given their position in the social network. Of particular interest is the minimum *number* of agents needed to trigger a shift from one norm to another (say through a targeted intervention) and who those agents might be. It turns out that it is sometimes sufficient for a *single* agent to switch (and stay switched) for the entire population to shift through a process of contagion. Moreover, contrary to what one might think, it is not necessarily the well-connected agents who are best placed to induce change: in some cases peripheral, poorly connected agents are the ones that are in the best position to promote norm shifts, a point that has been documented empirically.[7]

This phenomenon can be illustrated very simply by the example shown in Figure 5.7. The weights on every edge around the ring equal 1, whereas the weight on every edge from the hub is worth a little less, namely 0.9. The interpretation is that interactions with one's immediate neighbors around the ring are a bit stronger than interactions with the more distant hub. The payoff

[6] For empirical studies of tipping points see Centola 2018, Centola et al. 2018, and Andreoni et al. 2021.

[7] For a discussion of this phenomenon with empirical examples see Centola 2018, 2021, 2024. Topological properties of networks that promote contagion are discussed by Morris 2000.

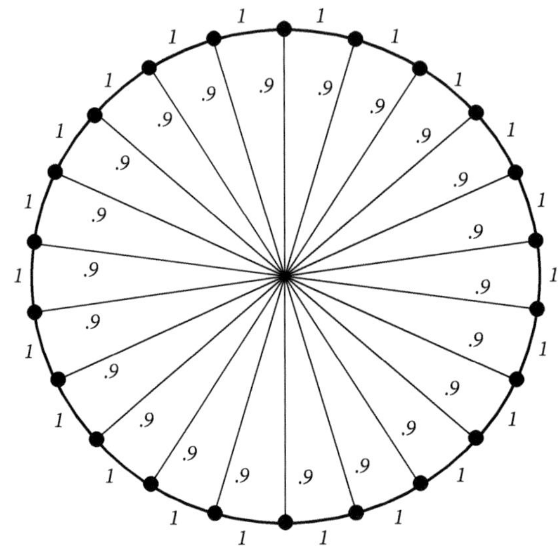

Figure 5.7 Hub and spokes network with weighted edges. Tipping occurs on the periphery more readily than at the center.

from interacting with a neighbor is equal to its weight times the corresponding payoff in the following game matrix:

	A	B	
A	2, 2	0, 0	(8)
B	0, 0	1, 1	

Suppose the process starts in the state where everyone is playing B. If any single agent on the ring could be induced to switch from B to A, then it is a best reply for his immediate neighbors on the ring to switch to A, then for their neighbors to switch to A, and so forth around the ring. The agent at the hub will only switch when at least one-third of the ring agents have switched. By contrast, if initially the hub agent could be induced to switch to A, this would not be sufficient to induce any of the other agents to switch. In short, the tipping number is 1, and the agents who trigger the tip are peripheral and poorly connected. This phenomenon clearly extends well beyond this particular example. An agent with few neighbors is inherently more susceptible to being flipped than is an agent with many neighbors. If the poorly connected agents form a suitably connected subnetwork, just one such agent can trigger a norm switch among all of them, leading to a norm switch among all the agents.

In summary, this chapter has shown that the speed of transitions between equilibria is crucially dependent on the amount of random variation in agents' behaviors as well as on the network structure through which they interact. When the variance is large enough, the expected transition time can be surprisingly short even when the population is large and everyone interacts equally with everyone else. Other classes of networks exhibit even faster transition times, and in some cases it takes only a few agents (not necessarily the best-connected ones) to instigate a norm shift in the entire population.

6

Norms of Compensation in Share Contracts

6.1 Customary contracts

How much should I pay a tort lawyer who is representing me in a workplace injury case? Conventional economic theory suggests that the terms we agree to should reflect the lawyer's track record, the likelihood of winning in court, the potential amount of compensation, our attitudes toward risk, the option of going to another lawyer, and so forth. It follows that the outcome will be idiosyncratic to our personal characteristics and circumstances. One would therefore expect to find a significant degree of dispersion in the agreed terms across many different cases. But in fact my lawyer will probably stipulate that she get one-third of any settlement because this is the usual and customary contingency fee, and I will probably agree to it.[1]

This phenomenon is by no means limited to legal fees. Money managers typically charge standard rates as a percentage of the amount under management, architects charge a standard percentage of the cost of construction, real estate agents take a standard percentage of the sales price of a house, landlords give their tenants a customary share of the crops they produce, hedge fund managers earn a standard bonus over and above a benchmark level of return, and so forth.

The theory of norms can help us make sense of this *excess uniformity* or *compression effect*, which states that the force of custom suppresses the dispersion of outcomes that one would expect given the differences in agents' preferences, circumstances, and outside options that should matter in a traditional neoclassical model. The theory also illuminates several other features of such contractual arrangements that are poorly accounted for by standard theory. One feature is that customary fees and shares tend to be "sticky": when underlying economic conditions change, say regarding the supply and demand for a given service, standard terms tend to be slow to adjust. A second feature

This chapter is based in part on Young and Burke 2001.

[1] In a survey of contingency fees in Wisconsin, Kritzer 2004, p. 39, found that in about 60% of the cases the shares were one-third for the lawyer, two-thirds for the client except for states where the fees are regulated by statute.

The Dynamics of Social Norms. H. Peyton Young, Oxford University Press.
 DOI: 10.1093/oso/9780198959052.003.0006

is that uniformity is often framed in terms of round numbers that act as focal points. (The standard lawyer's contingency fee is 1/3, not for example 11/31). A third feature is that uniformity is sometimes localized: contractual customs may differ markedly between different geographical regions (the local conformity, global diversity effect). Fourth, excess uniformity can have nontrivial economic consequences because it distorts factor returns.

What, though, are the incentives that give rise to such contractual norms? I argue that there are two main mechanisms. One is that contractual norms are based on powerful focal points that make bargaining easier and thereby reduce transaction costs. This is reflected in the use of round numbers, such as 20% for hedge fund bonuses, one-third for tort lawyers, 50:50 division among farmers, and so forth. A second and more subtle mechanism is that departure from customary practice suggests an inattentiveness to norms and customs more generally. In an environment where contracts are incomplete, this sends a negative signal to one's counterparty, who wants to be confident that you will not haggle over every unforeseen detail and contingency that might arise in the course of the relationship. By adhering to a prevailing contractual norm, both parties signal that they are inclined to follow norms and are therefore predictable and easy to deal with.

In this chapter I shall illustrate these points using several concrete examples, including real estate commissions, hedge fund fees, and cropsharing contracts in US agriculture. The latter case is especially interesting due to the detailed datasets on these contracts that have been collected by the US Department of Agriculture. In particular, the data allow one to estimate the extent to which the net payments to principals and agents are distorted by the normative character of the contracts.[2]

6.2 Real estate commissions

In the United States, the standard (modal) commission for selling a house is 6%, which is paid by the seller, and this has been the case for many years. The rate is a "norm" in the sense that it is customary and expected. A homeowner who approaches an agent about selling her house will almost invariably be quoted 6% as the going rate, irrespective of the value of the house. It turns out that this percentage (which is not particularly "round"), dates to the 1940s, when it was fixed by the National Association of Realtors. Despite subsequent

[2] The focus of this chapter is on sharing norms between principals and agents. For a review of the role of social norms in labor markets more generally see Görges and Nosenzo 2020.

lawsuits and a Supreme Court decision that declared the practice to be anti-competitive,[3] local real estate boards continued to "suggest" 6% without fixing it outright.

Negotiation around the normal commission occurs to some extent, of course, but in most cases the broker won't concede much. Moreover, there is a powerful argument against making too much of a concession: the house will be shown by agents from other firms, and the commission will be divided equally between the listing agent and the one who concludes the sale. (Equal division between listing and selling agent is another example of a contractual norm.) A lower commission therefore reduces the incentive of other brokers to show the house to prospective buyers, so it is not necessarily in the interest of the seller to negotiate a lower rate. A lower rate might also be taken as a signal that the broker must undercut the market in order to attract business, and hence is inferior in quality.

6.3 Hedge fund commissions

Another contemporary example of a sharing norm can be seen in the hedge fund industry. Until very recently, the standard was to charge "two and twenty": 2% per year in management fees, and 20% of the profit earned over and above some established benchmark rate of return. Where did this arrangement come from? It turns out that it too is embedded in precedent. Alfred Winslow Jones, who originated the concept of hedge funds in the 1940s, charged a 20% performance fee and claimed as justification that this was the rate charged by Phoenician merchants in ancient times.[4] In spite of the proliferation of funds and the huge growth in assets under management since then, this particular commission structure remained the industry norm for many years. Although fees have eroded somewhat, a 20% performance bonus was until recently by far the most common rate (see Figure 6.1).

This distribution has three noteworthy features:

i) it is "spiky"—just six rates account for over 96% of the reported values (*the quantum effect*)
ii) the spikes occur at "round" numbers (*the focal point effect*)
iii) the historical rate of 20% is still the most common (*persistence*).

[3] United States v. Real Estate Boards 1950.
[4] Mallaby 2010, p. 30.

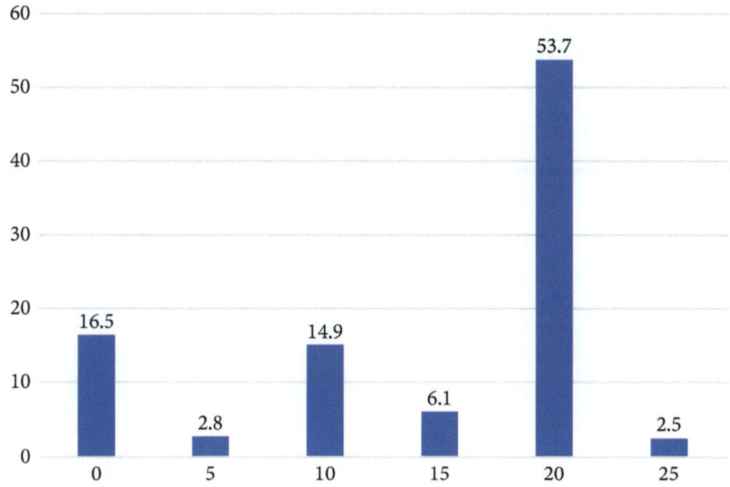

Figure 6.1 Frequency distribution of hedge fund performance fees in 2018.
Source: Vikas Agarwal, private communication.

As previously noted, these features follow naturally from the theory of norms, but they are not well accounted for by conventional contract theory.

6.4 Cropsharing contracts

A contractual norm that has long attracted the attention of economists is cropsharing in agriculture.[5] In its most basic form, a cropsharing contract specifies the division of output for a landowner and the tenant who farms the land. The logic of a share contract is that it shares the risk of an uncertain outcome between the landowner and the tenant while offering the latter an incentive to increase the expected value of that outcome. According to standard principal–agent theory, the size of the tenant's share should reflect such factors as the tenant's ability, the inherent productivity of the land, the risk aversion of the contracting parties, their outside options, and so forth.[6] It seems reasonable to suppose that such factors vary substantially from one pair of contracting agents to another, in which case the outcomes should exhibit substantial dispersion. In actual practice, however, the agreed shares tend to cluster around "usual and customary" levels even when there are substantial and observable differences in the inherent productivity of different parcels of land, as well as

[5] Smith 1976 [1776], Mill 1848, Marshall 1890.
[6] Cheung 1969, Stiglitz 1974, Bolton and Dewatripont 2005.

differences in ability among the tenants (the "compression effect"). Furthermore, these contractual norms tend to be anchored at prominent focal points, such as 1/2–1/2, 2/5–3/5, or 1/3–2/3.

The importance of such focal points, and the fact that they tend to be specific and long-lasting within particular regions, has been documented in many parts of the world, including India, Africa, and the United States.[7] John Stuart Mill called attention to the normative aspect of share contracts in the case of Italian agriculture in his day:

> This proportion [for the landlord] . . . is usually (as is implied by the words *metayer*, *mezzaiuolo*, and *medietarius*) one-half. There are places, however, such as the rich volcanic soil of the province of Naples, where the landlord takes two-thirds . . . Whether the proportion is two-thirds or one-half, it is a fixed proportion, not variable from farm to farm, or from tenant to tenant.[8]

The reader may be surprised to learn that cropsharing is still one of the most common contract forms even in advanced agricultural economies such as the United States. In the remainder of this chapter, I shall study the terms of these contracts in depth, using survey data for the state of Illinois collected by the US Department of Agriculture over the period 1977 to 1994. These data provide detailed information on the terms of contracts on several thousand farms in different parts of the state, including the size of each farm, the terms on which all inputs and outputs are shared, the output per acre, and the net incomes to tenant and landlord.

The first point to note is that very few fractional divisions of the output are actually used: over 98% of the cropshare contracts stipulate a landlord–tenant division of 1/2–1/2, 2/5–3/5, or 1/3–2/3. Second, there are strong regional differences in their frequency of use. Illinois consists of two regions that differ in their soil characteristics and geology. In the north, the land is flat and the soils are, on average, highly productive. In the south, the land is hillier, the topsoil is not as thick, and on average it is less productive (see Figure 6.2).[9] In the northern part of the state the customary share for the tenant is 1/2, whereas in the southern part of the state the customary share is either 3/5 or 2/3 (see Figure 6.3). In the South, the higher tenant's share

[7] Bardhan and Rudra 1980, Bardhan 1984, Robertson 1987.

[8] Mill 1848, p. 303.

[9] The north–south divide is determined by the southern boundary of the last major glaciation (the Wisconsin glaciation), which ended about twelve thousand years ago (Mausel et al. 1975).

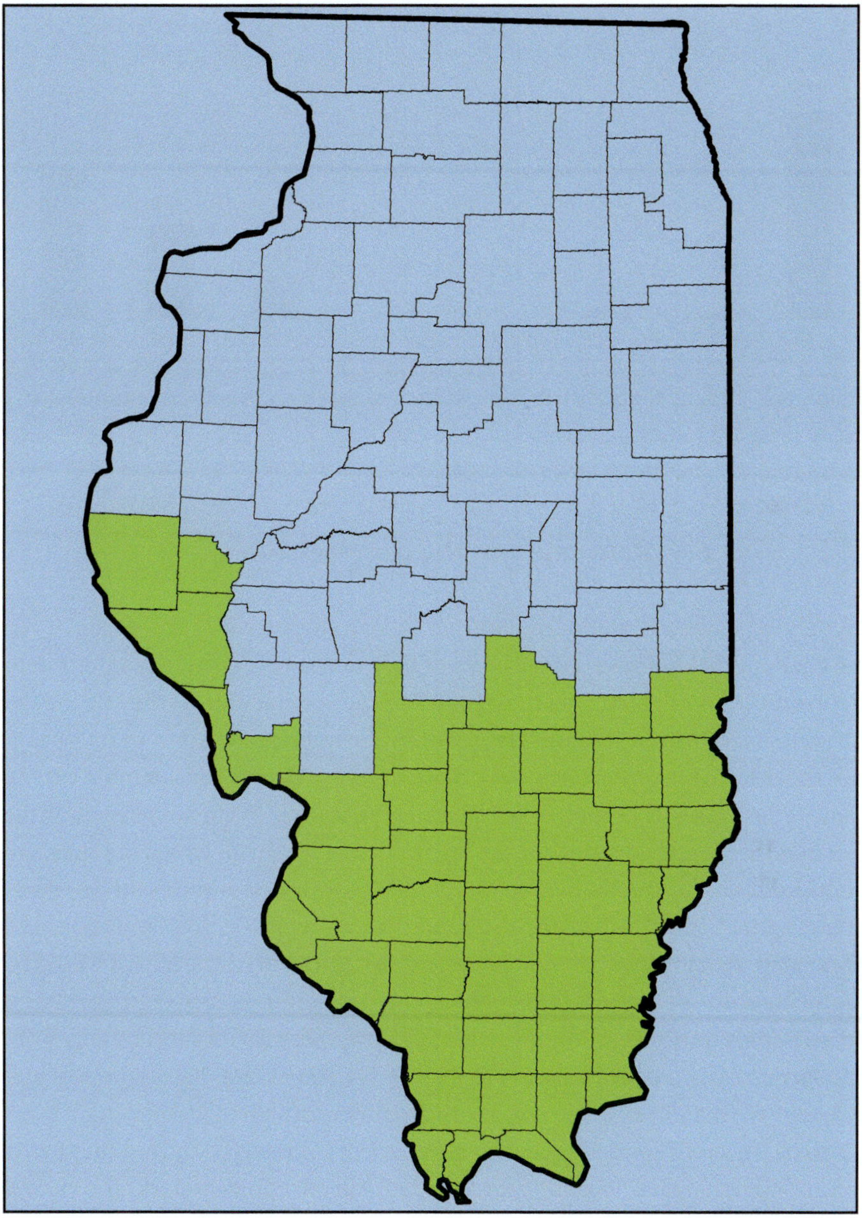

Figure 6.2 Illinois counties in the northern and southern regions (shaded).

compensates for the poorer land quality. This is an example of the *local conformity/global diversity* effect.[10]

[10] It is conceivable that higher tenant shares in the south are needed to attract tenants due to higher wages in the non-agricultural sector. It turns out, however, that non-agricultural wages in the south are actually lower than in the north (Burke 2015).

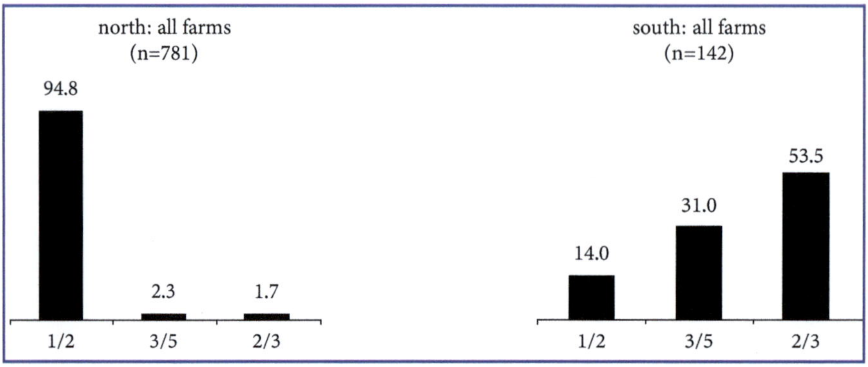

Figure 6.3 Tenant share distribution in the northern and southern counties.
Source: Young and Burke 2001, Figure 3.

6.5 Rent capture: the compression effect

As previously noted, standard contract theory suggests that heterogeneity in the characteristics and circumstances of the contracting parties should lead to a corresponding degree of heterogeneity in the contract terms they negotiate. In actuality, however, the high degree of uniformity observed in practice suggests that local custom overpowers these differences to a considerable extent. Can we test for this compression effect empirically? To do so we exploit the fact that the data report the *soil quality index* of each farm, which is a measure of the inherent productivity of the land under controlled amounts of labor and other inputs.[11] In a purely competitive market, more productive land should be associated with lower shares for the tenant since otherwise the tenant would be capturing some of the rent that ought to accrue to land. In fact, contract shares are strikingly uniform locally even though soil quality varies substantially from one farm to the next. For example, Figure 6.4 shows the distribution of soil indexes (horizontal axis) corresponding to different shares for the tenant (vertical axis) in a representative county in the north (Tazewell), and another in the south (Effingham). The results for Tazewell are particularly stark: the richest farms are twice as productive as the poorest farms (as measured by expected yield per acre), yet almost all operate under the same share (1/2–1/2). The implication is that, due to the rigidity of the sharing norm, tenants on the richest farms could be earning up to twice the income of tenants on the poorest

[11] Odell and Oschwald 1970, Fehrenbacher et al. 1978.

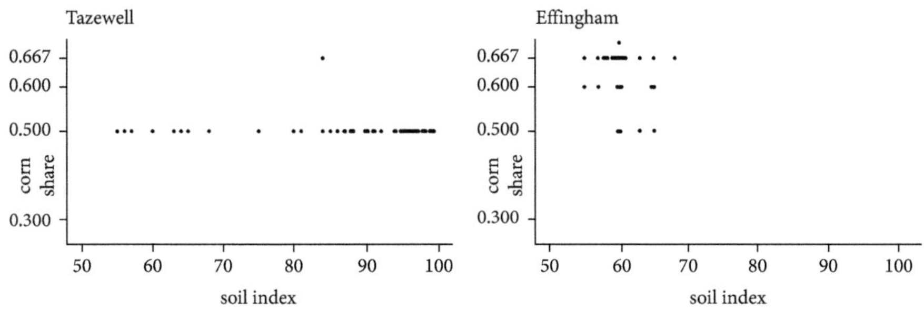

Figure 6.4 Distribution of shares in a representative northern county (Tazewell, left panel) and a representative southern county (Effingham, right panel) as a function of soil quality.
Source: Young and Burke 2001, Figure 5.

farms in the region without putting in any extra effort or additional inputs such as seed, fertilizer, and herbicides.

The Illinois data is sufficiently detailed that one can test for this possibility econometrically. In particular, one can exploit the fact that the soil index is calibrated so that it measures the expected yield per acre on soils of a given type, holding fixed the amount of labor and other inputs. If tenants are putting in extra effort and/or more inputs on higher quality land (or if higher quality land tends to attract higher-ability tenants due to assortative matching), then observed yields should increase more rapidly than is predicted by the corresponding increase in the soil quality index. Burke (2015) shows, however, that this is not the case: actual yields increase at a rate that is consistent with the calibrated yields under controlled levels of inputs.

Another way of examining whether sharing norms are distorting factor returns is to compare observed yields on farms with the *same* level of soil quality but that operate on different share contracts. As Figure 6.4 shows, there is a significant overlap in the range of soil qualities between northern and southern farms. Many farms in the south with soil quality index in the range 55–65 give 2/3 or 3/5 to the tenant, whereas farms of similar quality in the north give 1/2 to the tenant. If the higher share in the south induces greater effort by the tenant, or attracts more able tenants, the yields in the south should be greater than those on comparable farms in the north. As Burke shows, this is not the case either: observed yields on higher-share farms in the south are actually somewhat *lower* than on northern farms of comparable soil quality that operate on a lower tenant share. Due to share rigidity, tenants on above-average quality farms in the south are apparently able to free-ride on the prevailing high tenant share in the south without putting in more labor (or non-labor) inputs compared to tenants working on farms in the north of comparable quality (the *excess diversity* effect).

Note, however, that although factor returns may be distorted from their purely competitive levels, this does not necessarily imply a loss in welfare. A contractual norm is a form of social capital that reduces transaction costs for both principal and agent, and is especially valuable in situations where contracts are incomplete and returns are highly unpredictable.

6.6 The dynamics of contractual norms

The evolutionary framework developed in Chapter 3 can help explain the distortion in factor returns that is attributable to contractual norms, as well as the regional character of these norms. Let us assume that the terms of the share contract adopted at a specific farm i depend on three factors: the farm's inherent productivity (yield per acre), local wages from non-agricultural employment, and the frequency with which the contract is used by others in the vicinity. (I am leaving aside such issues as heterogeneity in the parties' risk aversion and rates of time preference.) Let θ_i denote the expected output of farm i under a standard management regime with controlled levels of inputs, and let w_i denote the annual wage available to the tenant from alternative employment. A *share contract* at i specifies a share x_i for the tenant, and the complementary share $1 - x_i$ for the landlord, where $x_i \in [0, 1]$.[12] The tenant's expected annual income on farm i is $\theta_i x_i$, and the landlord's is $\theta_i(1 - x_i)$. The *incentive-compatible* contracts are those that induce the tenant to accept farm employment instead of the alternative wage w_i, that is, they satisfy the constraint $\theta_i x_i \geq w_i$.

To model the impact of local custom, let us suppose that farms are situated at the vertices of a graph, and that two farms are *neighbors* if and only if there is an edge joining them. Assume for simplicity that all edge-weights equal one. Thus, all neighbors of a given farm i have an equal degree of social influence on the contracting parties at i. For analytical convenience I shall assume that the set of feasible contracts X is finite; an example is $X = \{0, 0.1, 0.2, \ldots, 0.9, 1.0\}$. Let $X_i = \{x_i \in X : \theta_i x_i \geq w_i\}$ denote the set of incentive-compatible contracts at i.

[12] Shares are applied to the physical output (measured in bushels), which translates into gross income by multiplying the output by the current price per bushel.

A *state* of the process at a given time t is a vector $\boldsymbol{x}(t) \in \prod_i X_i$ that specifies the contract in force at each farm. (For simplicity I shall omit the dependence on t in the following discussion.) Let us assume that the landlord offers the tenant a contract, which the latter accepts provided it does not violate the incentive-compatibility constraint. As in Chapter 3, let us assume that the landlord's utility function on farm i is additively separable in individual and social utility:

$$U_i(\boldsymbol{x}) = u_i(x_i) + \lambda \sum_{j \in N_i} s(x_i, x_j). \tag{1}$$

Here N_i is the set of i's neighbors, $s(x_i, x_j)$ is the social utility to i from a neighbor whose contract is x_j, and λ measures the relative strength of social versus private utility. For simplicity, let us assume that the landlord's private utility is equal to his *rental income* $r_i(x_i)$, that is,

$$u_i(x_i) = r_i(x_i) = \theta_i(1 - x_i). \tag{2}$$

In general, the social utility $s(x_i, x_j)$ may depend (perhaps nonlinearly) on the size of the gap $x_j - x_i$, as well as on its sign. In the cropsharing application, the data suggests that *exact* coordination is of primary importance, rather than the size of the gap between the neighbors' shares and one's own, because one almost never sees small deviations around the norm. (In Illinois, for example, almost all shares are multiples of 1/2, 1/3 or 1/5.)[13] There is a benefit to choosing exactly the same share as one's neighbors, because this reduces transaction costs and also signals sensitivity to norms in general, which is important when contracts are incomplete.

We can represent this situation by a delta-function as follows:

$$\begin{aligned} \delta(x_i, x_j) &= 1 \quad \text{if } x_i = x_j \\ \delta(x_i, x_j) &= 0 \quad \text{if } x_i \neq x_j \end{aligned} \tag{3}$$

With these assumptions we obtain the following utility function for the landlord at location i:

$$U_i(\boldsymbol{x}) = \theta_i(1 - x_i) + \lambda \sum_{j \in N_i} \delta(x_i, x_j). \tag{4}$$

[13] The use of simple fractions has been documented in other countries where cropsharing is common (Bardhan and Rudra 1980, Robertson 1987). Recall Mill's observation that in Italy the fractions for the tenant were either 1/2 or 1/3 depending on the region.

Since the delta function is symmetric, this is a potential game. Let $r(\boldsymbol{x}) = \sum_i \theta_i(1 - x_i)$ denote the total rent to land in state $\boldsymbol{x}$, and let $c(\boldsymbol{x}) = (1/2)\sum_{i,j} \delta_{ij}(\boldsymbol{x})$ denote the number of (unordered) neighbor-pairs that are coordinated on the same contract. A potential function for this dynamical system can be expressed in the compact form

$$\rho(\boldsymbol{x}) = r(\boldsymbol{x}) + \lambda c(\boldsymbol{x}). \tag{5}$$

We know from chapter 3 that when deviations from best response follow a logit distribution, the stochastic dynamical system has an especially transparent ergodic distribution, namely, the long-run probability of each state $\boldsymbol{x}$ is proportional to $e^{\beta\rho(\boldsymbol{x})}$ for some non-negative scalar β (see Proposition 3.1). Hence the stochastically stable states are precisely those that maximize the total rent to land plus the total amount of coordination.

Although this model is highly simplified, it provides useful insights; in particular, it explains why behavior tends to coalesce into regional rather than global norms. To illustrate, consider the following hypothetical example. There are 32 farms, each of which has soil quality High, Medium, or Low as shown in Figure 6.5. The expected yield for each type of soil is: High 10, Medium 8, Low 6. For the 16 "northern" farms the yields are a mix of 10 and 8, whereas for the 16 "southern" farms they are a mix of 8 and 6.

Suppose that the salient shares can be expressed in multiples of 10%. Suppose further that the tenant's alternative wage is 4, that is, he will accept no

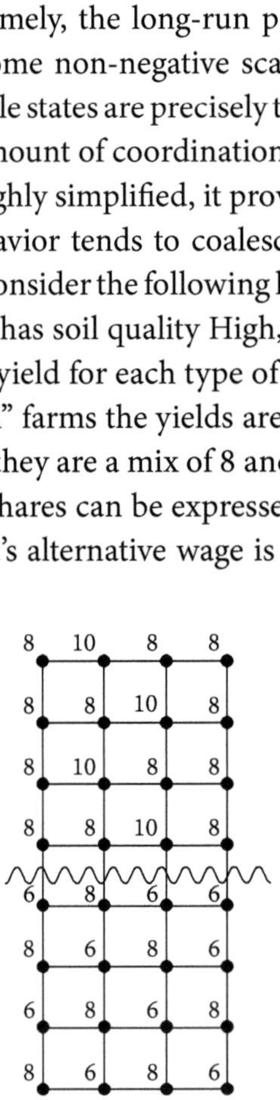

Figure 6.5 A spatial arrangement of farms with three soil qualities: 10, 8, 6. The northern farms are the upper 16 and the southern farms are the lower 16.

contract that yields less. Thus the minimum acceptable share for the tenant on low quality soils is 70%, on medium quality soils it is 50%, and on high quality soils it is 40%. The equilibria depend on the magnitude of the social coefficient λ. The simplest case arises when $\lambda = 0$, that is, there is no benefit to coordinating with one's neighbors. In this situation the landlord's objective is to maximize her returns subject to keeping her tenant from accepting alternative employment. The unique equilibrium is: High 40%, Medium 50%, Low 70%. This is the competitive outcome with no social spillover effects when the shares are constrained to be multiples of 10%.

Now suppose that $\lambda = 1$. The competitive outcome is no longer an equilibrium. For example, landlords on high-quality farms in the north would be better off by offering their tenants 50% instead of 40%, because the increased coordination with neighboring medium-quality farms more than offsets the loss in rental income. Similarly, in the south, landlords on medium-quality farms would be better off by offering their tenants 70% instead of 50%, because they gain more in coordination payoffs than they give up in rent.

Now consider the situation where all farms in the north offer 50% and all farms in the south offer 70%. Given the spatial distribution of soil qualities in Figure 6.5, this arrangement constitutes an equilibrium. Note in particular that medium-quality farms in the south earn substantially less rent than identical farms in the north. This is due to the distorting effect of the local norm. (Recall from Figure 6.4 that substantial differences actually do exist for farms of similar quality located in different regions.) This *excess diversity* is the flip side of *excess uniformity*. Within a given region individuals act similarly even though they are different, whereas in different regions individuals act differently even though they are similar.

The regional norm 50% north/70% south is not, however, the only equilibrium. In fact, it can be checked that 60% north/70% south is also an equilibrium, as is 70% everywhere (though the latter is not a strict equilibrium.) Which of these equilibria are most likely to emerge in the long run? In this case the answer turns out to be the regional norm 50/70. As compared to the 60/70 outcome, 50/70 increases the rent to land while keeping the total amount of coordination fixed, so it has higher potential. As compared to the 70/70 outcome, 50/70 increases the rent to land by $.2 \times 10 \times 4 + .2 \times 8 \times 12 = 27.2$ while decreasing the number of coordinated edges by 4. Hence the regional norm 50/70 has higher potential; moreover, it can be verified that it has highest potential among all feasible states.

6.7 Qualitative features of the dynamics

The preceding discussion highlights certain qualitative features of the dynamics that hold at a fairly general level. When the coordination motive is fairly strong (but not too strong), regional norms will tend to form that reflect *average* conditions within each region. In particular, regions with high average soil quality will tend to offer lower shares to the tenant, just as would be predicted by a competitive model absent social spillover effects. The reason is that distinct regions tend to have relatively few linkages that cross the boundary between them, which reduces the incentive to coordinate between people who are on opposite sides of the boundary. The result is a high degree of conformity within each region in spite of heterogeneity in land quality within the region, and substantial differences between regions that reflect differences in their average conditions. Norms create excess uniformity within regions, and excess diversity between similar individuals in different regions. As Figures 6.3 and 6.4 show, both of these features are borne out by the contract data in Illinois. Data on the soil quality of individual farms allows an assessment of the extent to which factor returns from their competitive values. Controlling for the quality of factor inputs in other cases where norms seem to be operating, such as professional fees in law, real estate, or finance, is a challenge that calls out for more empirical research.

7
Costly Norms

with Sam Jindani

7.1 The dynamics of costly norms

Costly norms are pervasive in many societies. Historical examples include dueling in Europe and footbinding in China; contemporary examples include female genital cutting in parts of Africa, and norms of conspicuous consumption more or less everywhere. Adhering to such norms can be very costly for individuals, but deviating has such negative social consequences that it is better to bear the cost. In this chapter I shall consider several examples of costly norms with a particular focus on their intermediate-run dynamics. Some persist for a long time and then die out suddenly, as was the case for dueling in England and footbinding in China. Others transition to an intermediate state before disappearing, as was the case for dueling in France. Another pattern, which is characteristic of norms of conspicuous consumption, is gradual escalation followed by sudden collapse.

Here I shall examine the reasons for these patterns using the framework developed in earlier chapters. A key difference from the previous analysis is to consider forms of social interaction that are more complex than simple measures of disparity from others' actions. In particular, I shall consider social penalties (and rewards) that depend on the *direction* and *extent* of deviations from what others are doing. Due to this asymmetry, the underlying game may not be representable by a potential function, and the dynamics can be quite complex, as we shall soon see.

7.2 Dueling

Early one morning in 1804, Alexander Hamilton and Aaron Burr left Manhattan in separate boats and rowed across the Hudson River to New Jersey. At

This chapter is an abbreviated version of Jindani and Young 2026.

The Dynamics of Social Norms. H. Peyton Young with Sam Jindani, Oxford University Press.
 DOI: 10.1093/oso/9780198959052.003.0007

the time, dueling was outlawed in many states and it was common for New Yorkers to duel in New Jersey because the ban there was less strictly enforced. Pistols were usually hidden in a bag, allowing the rowers to declare under oath that they had not seen them; they also faced away from the duelists. Although Hamilton was morally opposed to dueling and felt that it would be irresponsible toward his wife and children to risk his life, he decided to go ahead with the duel anyway, because of the public discredit that would ensue from refusing Burr's challenge. On the day of the duel, Hamilton missed, perhaps intentionally; Burr hit and mortally wounded Hamilton, who died the following day.[1]

Dueling is a particularly stark example of a costly social norm. Even though it was illegal in many jurisdictions, people felt compelled to play their part, especially members of the military and professional classes such as lawyers and politicians. Contemporary accounts make it clear that reputational concerns were the primary consideration: people feared the loss of standing among their peers if they failed to challenge someone to a duel when one was expected, or failed to accept a challenge, or in any way breached the norms surrounding dueling, and this concern was sufficient to drive them to risk their lives. A striking illustration of the norm's power are the numerous instances of people participating in a duel despite being opposed to the practice, including Hamilton.[2]

Costly social norms are rarely all or nothing: they are multi-dimensional and can assume many intermediate and nuanced forms. In the case of dueling, convention regulated when it was appropriate to challenge someone to a duel, how the duel should be organised, what type of weapons should be used, and so forth. Moreover, these conventions differed from place to place and changed over time. Until the mid-sixteenth century, duelists in France and England predominantly used slashing broadswords and protected themselves with bucklers. Eventually, broadswords were replaced by rapiers, which were far more deadly since they could more easily damage internal organs.[3] When pistols became popular in the late eighteenth century, subsidiary norms emerged concerning the distance separating the duelists. The conventional distance was 10 or 12 paces, which might be reduced if the duel was particularly serious, or increased if the converse was true.[4] Duelists who stood at

[1] Chernow 2004.
[2] Chernow 2004, p. 685.
[3] Stone 1965, pp. 242–244.
[4] Hopton 2007, pp. 30–33.

smaller distances were considered reckless;[5] those who stood further apart were considered cowardly; both were met with social opprobrium.

In England, dueling died out suddenly in the mid-nineteenth century, whereas in France it endured up to the turn of the century, albeit in a different form.[6] Swords became popular again, and, increasingly, the risks involved in dueling were made explicit, ranging from *au premier sang* to *à la mort*.[7] These changes had the effect of drastically reducing fatality rates. By the second half of the nineteenth century, only a small proportion of duels ended in the death of one of the duelists. Indeed, the change was so significant that duelists became the subject of ridicule, which hastened its demise as a symbol of masculine honor.[8]

7.3 Footbinding

Footbinding was prevalent for over a millennium in China, from the tenth century to the turn of the twentieth century, especially among the upper classes.[9] The procedure started around the age of six, before the arches of the feet were fully developed, and took years to complete. The feet were broken, folded on themselves, and bound tightly with bandages to mold them to the desired shape: a compressed arched foot around 10 centimeters in length. The bandages were redone and tightened regularly for the next 6 to 10 years. The whole procedure was extremely painful, and frequently led to infection. It is thought that as many as 10% of girls subjected to the process did not survive. Those who did were hobbled for life. However, the pressure to conform was considerable: bound feet were considered attractive, a sign of the family's wealth and status, and they enhanced a girl's marriage prospects.

As with dueling, there was variation in the norm across time and place. Remains from the thirteenth century show women with bound feet, but not as small as the later 10-centimeter ideal. There were also distinct regional variants, for instance in Sichuan, where people practiced a less severe form of footbinding that did not involve distorting the heel. Governments attempted to

[5] In a popular dueling manual, the Comte de Chatauvillard wrote that "honour might require us to risk our lives, but not to play with them" (Nye 1993, p. 142).

[6] Banks 2008, Hopton 2007, p. 323.

[7] Banks 2012, pp. 49–50.

[8] "Much as the modern French duel is ridiculed by certain smart people, it is in reality one of the most dangerous institutions of our day. Since it is always fought in the open air, the combatants are nearly sure to catch cold." Mark Twain 1880, *A Tramp Abroad*, p. 38.

[9] The following account is based on Mackie 1996, Ko 2007, and Gates 2015.

outlaw the practice on at least two occasions, in 1665 and 1847, but were unsuccessful. Toward the end of the nineteenth century, footbinding fell increasingly out of favor in public opinion, and it was condemned by Chinese intellectuals as being incompatible with modern Chinese society. “Natural foot” societies were formed whose members pledged not to bind their daughters’ feet and discouraged their sons from marrying girls with bound feet. The practice was officially banned in 1912 and outlawed still more forcefully under the Communist regime. As a result of these measures, as well as changing cultural norms, the practice had all but disappeared by the mid-twentieth century.

7.4 Conspicuous consumption: chopines and super-yachts

Norms of conspicuous consumption call for spending lavishly on goods and services whose main purpose is to display wealth and status.[10] A striking contemporary example is that of “super-yachts,” which are a means for the wealthiest members of society to distinguish themselves from the rest.[11] In the past 20 years, the average length of a luxury yacht has crept up from 60 to 80 meters. According to a Silicon Valley CEO, until recently “a 50-meter boat was considered a good-sized boat. Now that would be a little bit embarrassing.”[12] This view illustrates the normative aspect of conspicuous consumption: the desired level of consumption depends on what others are consuming.

A well-documented historical example was the fashion among wealthy women in Renaissance Venice for wearing platform shoes known as chopines. The height of the shoes symbolized the status of the wearer and allowed her to tower over others. Over time, chopines gradually increased in height until they became almost unwearable: some were over 50 centimeters tall and wearers required a servant to help them walk. Higher chopines also entailed a higher monetary cost, both because the shoes themselves were costlier and because the wearer would need longer dresses. In 1430, a law attempted to limit their height to three inches, but it was widely flouted.[13] Eventually, in the seventeenth century, chopines fell out of fashion as heels became more popular.[14]

[10] “With the greater part of rich people, the chief enjoyment of riches consists in the parade of riches.” Smith 1976 [1776], Book I, p. 190. The term “conspicuous consumption” was coined by Veblen 1899.

[11] Osnos 2022.

[12] Cited by Osnos 2022.

[13] The pervasiveness of sumptuary laws, which regulated expenditure on certain kinds of luxury goods, demonstrates the extent to which conspicuous consumption was considered problematic, especially in cases where the luxury goods were imported (Riello and Rublack 2019).

[14] Bossan 2012, p. 35.

7.5 Varieties of costly norm dynamics

The preceding examples of costly norms display several noteworthy features. First, they are persistent: some endured for centuries despite repeated attempts to extirpate them. Second, they can assume alternative forms over time, which can be more or less costly. Third, adherence to the norm is motivated by the reputational consequences of a deviation, which are not necessarily symmetrical in the direction of the deviation. In the case of conspicuous consumption, for example, people may lose status if they consume too little, but they may also lose status if they consume too much, because they are disparaged as vulgar, insecure, or trying too hard. Fourth, the dynamics of costly norms are highly varied. Dueling in England died out quite suddenly, as did footbinding in China, whereas dueling in France transitioned to an intermediate, less costly norm before disappearing. By contrast, it appears that norms of conspicuous consumption often escalate gradually and then abruptly collapse.

In the remainder of this chapter, I shall show how these patterns can be explained in terms of the interpretation placed on deviations from a given social norm, and the attendant social cost. As in previous chapters, I shall consider a finite population of individuals who interact over time. Each agent chooses an action that has a private cost, and experiences a social cost that increases with the discrepancy between own and others' actions. From time to time, agents revise their choices by selecting a best response given the current actions of others. Unlike in previous chapters, the focus here will be on the specific form of the social cost function, and how it affects the intermediate-run dynamics. The model predicts that under some specifications, costly norms will tend to collapse suddenly (as was the case for dueling in England and footbinding in China), while under other conditions they will transition stepwise via lower-cost variants (as was the case for dueling in France). There are still other specifications of the social cost function that cause norms to escalate gradually before collapsing, which is a notable feature of episodes of conspicuous consumption.

7.6 Modeling the intermediate-run dynamics

Consider a finite population of m individuals, each of whom can choose an action from a finite set of feasible actions. Actions may be multi-dimensional. In the case of dueling, for example, individuals must decide what type of insult merits a challenge, where and when to conduct the duel, what type of weapon to use, whether to stand closer or further apart, and so forth. The *private cost* of action i will be denoted by c_i. For simplicity let us assume a one-to-one correspondence between actions and private costs, indexing them as follows: $0 = c_0 < c_1 < \cdots < c_n$. A *state* of the process is a vector $\boldsymbol{p} = (p_0, p_1, \ldots, p_n)$ that specifies the proportion of agents choosing each action. Since the population has m members, each component p_i is an integer multiple of $\delta = 1/m$. Let $s_{ij} = s(c_i, c_j)$ be the *social utility* induced by a j-player toward an i-player. The deterministic payoff to an i-player can be expressed as follows:

$$U_i(\boldsymbol{p}) = -c_i - \lambda \sum_j p_j s_{ij}. \tag{1}$$

Previous chapters focused on situations where the social utility function is symmetric, that is, $s_{ij} = s_{ji}$. This assumption has the advantage that the payoffs have the structure of a potential game, but it is not especially realistic in the current setting. Here I shall examine the various components of social utility in more detail and show how they affect the dynamics.

As in previous chapters, I define a *norm* to be a Nash equilibrium in which everyone plays the same action. Deviations from a prevailing norm may involve choosing a lower-cost action or a higher-cost action. Taking a lower-cost action has negative reputational consequences because it connotes cowardice, shirking, or inadequacy. However, reputational harm may also result from deviating too far in the other direction. For example, ostentatious displays of wealth may be viewed as a sign of insecurity, resulting in a loss of social status. Challenging someone to a duel over a petty dispute, or insisting on pistols when rapiers are the norm, may signal hot-headedness rather than bravery. In this way, reputational effects may restrain escalation toward costlier norms.

These considerations can be incorporated into a social utility function that is asymmetric. Given any nonnegative private costs c and c', let $s(c, c')$ denote the social utility of a c-player when interacting with a c'-player. (For simplicity, I shall identify actions with their private costs.) Starting at a norm where everyone's private cost is c', suppose that someone deviates to an action with cost $c \neq c'$. The deviation is *disincentivized* if $s(c, c') > 0$ and *incentivized* if $s(c, c') < 0$.

Figure 7.1 illustrates various possibilities. In the left-hand panel, all deviations are disincentivized. In the right-hand panel, cost increases ($c > c'$) are incentivized whereas cost decreases ($c < c'$) are disincentivized.

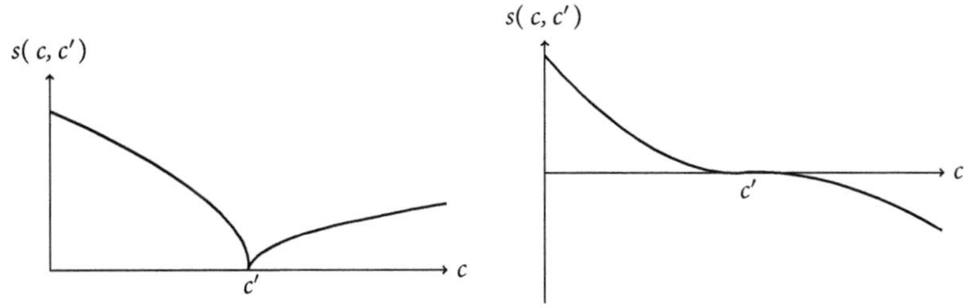

(a) Deviations are disincentivized and asymmetric in the direction of the deviation

(b) Deviations to more costly actions are incentivized; deviations to less costly actions are disincentivized

Figure 7.1 Different shapes of the social payoff function.

7.7 Disincentivized deviations: norm convergence and norm collapse

We know from Chapter 3 that if the agents' payoff functions define a potential game, then from any initial state there is a sequence of strict best responses that leads to a norm. In the present case, however, the game may not admit a potential function due to asymmetries in the social utilities. The dynamics can be quite complex: starting from a heterogenous state, an updating agent might choose a more costly action, a less costly action, and her preferred action might differ from those chosen by any of the other players. Nevertheless, it can be shown that when all deviations are disincentivized, the unperturbed strict best response process eventually converges to a norm from any initial state.

Proposition 7.1 *Suppose that all deviations are disincentivized. Then a norm exists and, from any initial state, the strict best response process converges almost surely in finite time to a norm.*[15]

When players occasionally deviate from best responses due to mistakes, misperceptions, or random payoff shocks, some norms will be much more likely to emerge than others in the long run, as was shown in previous chapters.[16] The focus of this chapter, by contrast, is on the intermediate rather than the long-run dynamics. It will be useful to begin by considering the behavior of the best-response dynamics without stochastic perturbations, and to show how

[15] This follows from Theorem 1 in Jindani and Young 2026.

[16] A general method for computing the stochastically stable norms is described in Young 1993a, 1998a.

they depend on the form of the social utility function. The analysis can be readily extended to incorporate stochastic perturbations that have very small probability, because in that case the stochastic dynamics over the intermediate run will follow a similar path to the deterministic best-response dynamic with high probability.[17]

I begin by examining the shape of the social payoff function in more detail. In many of the examples studied so far, norms are imbued with a meaning that communicates character, identity, or values. In these cases, even small departures from a prevailing norm may incur substantial social costs. Suppose, for example, that someone requests to duel at 11 paces when the conventional distance is 10. This may be interpreted as a sign of cowardice and treated in much the same way as a request to duel at 15 or 20 paces: they are "not the done thing." Similarly, in the case of conspicuous consumption, small differences can loom large: if someone owns a super-yacht that is only a few feet longer than everyone else's, they still have bragging rights about owning the biggest super-yacht.

We can capture the idea that small deviations have a relatively greater impact than large deviations by assuming that $s(c, c')$ is strictly concave in c for all $c < c'$ and for all $c > c'$, and also that $s(c, c')$ is strictly concave in c' for all $c' > c$ and for all $c' < c$. In this case, we shall say that the social utility function is *concave*. For example, in the left panel of Figure 7.1 social utility is concave, whereas in the right panel it is not.

The next result characterizes the dynamics of the process following societal changes that alter the relative importance of social versus private utility, as captured by the parameter λ. In particular, a change in λ may destabilize an existing norm and create a disequilibrium state in which everyone is playing the same action.

Proposition 7.2 *Suppose that deviations are disincentivized and the social utility function is concave. Starting from a disequilibrium state in which everyone is playing the same action, the strict best response process collapses directly to the costless norm.*

The idea of the proof is as follows. Recall that m is the number of agents and $\delta = 1/m$. Suppose the process begins in the state where everyone is playing

[17] This claim follows from results in stochastic approximation theory (Benaim and Weibull 2003).

action i but it is not an equilibrium. The payoff gain to a single agent who deviates to $j < i$ is

$$c_i - c_j - \lambda s_{ji}(1 - \delta) = (c_i - c_j)(1 - \lambda(1 - \delta)\bar{s}_{ji}) \tag{2}$$

where $\bar{s}_{ji} = s_{ji}/(c_i - c_j)$ strictly decreases as j decreases, due to concavity. Hence j=0 is the unique best response, so the first agent to revise chooses action 0. As the number of agents playing 0 increases (and the number playing i decreases), one can show that the payoff advantage of 0 goes up relative to all other alternatives. Hence the unravelling process continues until it reaches the absorbing state $\boldsymbol{p}^0$ where everyone plays action 0.

7.8 Stepwise de-escalation

When social utility is not concave, a reduction in the social multiplier λ may cause the process to transition to $\boldsymbol{p}^0$ through a series of intermediate actions known as "stepping stones."[18] This situation is easiest to analyze when there are just three alternatives, in which case there are simple necessary and sufficient conditions for stepwise de-escalation to occur.

Label the actions 0, 1, 2 where $0 = c_0 < c_1 < c_2$. Let $\boldsymbol{p}^i$ denote the state in which everyone is playing action i. Stepwise de-escalation means that, starting at $\boldsymbol{p}^2$, people switch from 2 to 1 until some point at which action 0 begins to increase, after which the process converges to $\boldsymbol{p}^0$. This pattern occurs when action 1 is the unique best response in state $\boldsymbol{p}^2$, and action 0 is the unique best response in state $\boldsymbol{p}^1$. These conditions imply, in particular, that

$$s_{02} > s_{01} + s_{12}. \tag{3}$$

Expression (3) is known as the *reverse triangle inequality*.[19] Notice that it holds for the social utility functions alone, and does not depend on the private utility functions. The reverse triangle inequality will be satisfied, for example, if the social pressure of 2-players against 1-players and of 1-players against 0-players are sufficiently small. Intuitively, action 1 must be a close social or symbolic substitute for both actions 0 and 2. The following example illustrates the best response dynamics in a particular case.

[18] Gulesci et al. 2025.
[19] Corollary 1 in Gulesci et al. 2025.

Example 7.1 Suppose there are three agents ($m = 3$) and three actions $i = 0, 1, 2$. Let $c_i = i$, $s(c, c') = 0$ for all $c \geq c'$, and $s(c, c') = (c' - c)^2$ for all $c < c'$. Suppose that the process starts at $\boldsymbol{p}^2$, that is, all agents are playing action 2. Let $\lambda = 2$ initially and then suppose it decreases to $\lambda' = 1$. We shall show that the process de-escalates via intermediate action 1.

At $\lambda = 2$, starting from $\boldsymbol{p}^2$, action 2 yields -2, action 1 yields $-1 - \lambda(2/3)(2-1)^2 = -7/3$ and action 0 yields $0 - \lambda(2/3)(2-0)^2 = -16/3$, hence agents have no incentive to deviate. However, at $\lambda' = 1$, action 1 yields $-1 - \lambda'(2/3)(2-1) = -5/3$, and action 0 yields $-0 - \lambda'(2/3)(2-0)^2 = -8/3$, so agents have an incentive to switch to 1. After one agent switches, it can be checked that action 1 remains the unique best response for all players, hence any revising agent will choose 1. Once a single agent remains at 2, 0 becomes a best response for that agent. Continuing in this way, the process converges to $\boldsymbol{p}^0$. Figure 7.2 illustrates the path of the process; the dots indicate the number of agents choosing each action in each period.

An historical example of stepwise de-escalation is the transition to much less costly forms of dueling in nineteenth-century France. A contemporary example is female genital circumcision (FGC) in Somalia, where a transition is currently underway from a very invasive, medically risky form of the practice known as Pharaonic, to a less harmful variant known as Sunna. The question is whether Sunna will serve as a stepping stone to eventual abandonment, or whether it will become entrenched as a new norm. The dynamics of this case are treated in detail in the next chapter, and the reverse triangle inequality turns out to play an important role in assessing which trajectory will eventually be realized.

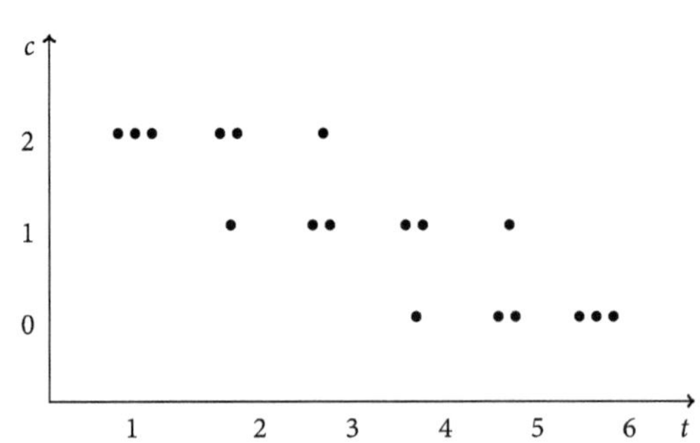

Figure 7.2 Stepwise de-escalation for the parameters in Example 7.1.

7.9 Escalation and collapse: conspicuous consumption

I turn now to the case of conspicuous consumption, where an additional motive must be considered, namely the desire to outdo others (*oneupmanship*). A billionaire takes satisfaction in owning a yacht that is larger than another's just as a Venetian lady feels superior if she wears higher chopines. Oneupmanship incentivizes costly deviations from the norm rather than discouraging them, and therefore plays the role of an *anti-coordination* motive. These considerations change the dynamics significantly. In particular, the process may not converge to a norm, but exhibit a recurring pattern of escalation and collapse, as we often see in episodes of conspicuous consumption.

To understand this phenomenon, it is instructive to think about the interaction of the various forces incentivizing and disincentivizing deviations in a concrete case. Suppose that one billionaire buys a yacht that is larger than those in his social group. On the one hand he derives pleasure from outdoing others, and doing so within moderation increases his social status. On the other hand, he needs to be wary of going too far, since that might be interpreted as a sign of insecurity. This is not the end of the matter however: his larger yacht causes others to feel inferior, which induces them to order still larger yachts in order to regain status and avoid invidious comparisons. The result is gradual escalation. Eventually, however, the expense becomes so great that giving up the status race altogether may actually be more attractive than climbing one more rung up the status ladder, in which case the norm quickly collapses. The following example illustrates these dynamics.

Example 7.2 Suppose there are three agents ($m = 3$), seven actions ($i = 0, 1, 2, 3, 4, 5, 6$), $c_i = i$, and $\lambda = 1$. Let $s(c, c) = 0$,

$$s(c, c') = 6 \text{ for } c < c' \text{ and } s(c, c') = -2 \text{ for } c > c'. \tag{4}$$

Suppose the process starts in the state where everyone is playing action 0. A revising agent gets 0 from staying at 0 and $-1 + (2/3)\,2 = 1/3$ from switching to 1. Switching to $i > 1$ yields $-i + (2/3)2 = -i + 4/3 < 1/3$. Hence the updating agent will switch to 1. In the new state, the agent at 1 has no incentive to switch; an agent at 0 gets $0 - (1/3)6 = -2$ from staying at 0, $-1 + (1/3)2 = -1/3$ from switching to 1, and $-2 + (2/3)2 = -2/3$ from switching to 2. Hence an agent will switch from 0 to 1. Continuing in this way, the path of the process is as shown in Figure 7.3.

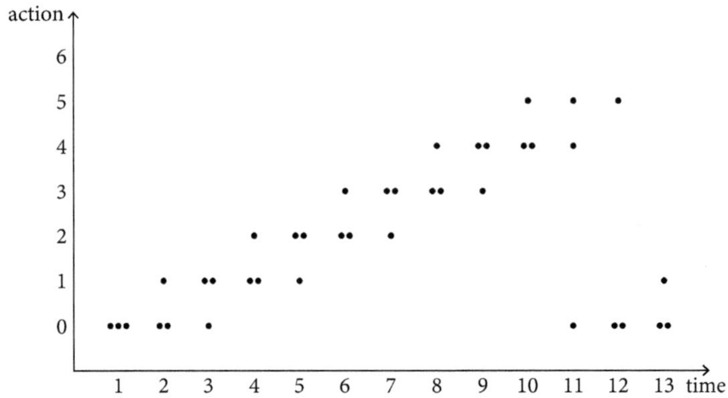

Figure 7.3 With the oneupmanship motive, the process can cycle.

Once the process reaches the state in period 10, one of the agents playing action 4 has an incentive to switch to 0. To see why, note that staying at 4 yields −4 −(6/3) = −6, switching to 5 yields −5 + (1/3)2 = −13/3, and switching to 6 yields −6 + (2/3)2 = −14/3, whereas switching to 0 yields −4. Once an agent has switched down to 0, the remaining agent at 4 has an incentive to follow. Finally, the agent at 5 has an incentive to switch to 1 once both other agents are at 0 (but not before). After this a new cycle will ensue, possibly with a different means of displaying one's wealth (e.g., diamonds in lieu of chopines, spaceships instead of yachts).

In general, the dynamics with oneupmanship can be significantly more complex than the example considered above and there may exist multiple best-response paths starting from a given state. It can be shown, however, that over a range of values that incentivize higher-cost deviations and disincentivize lower-cost deviations, the process will cycle and no stable norm exists.

7.10 Interventions

The social interactions model shows how different types of interventions can weaken a given costly norm. It also shows that some interventions may end up being counterproductive. One natural intervention would be to increase the costliness of a costly norm still further, say by taxing the activity. This intervention could tip the process into a lower cost variant; moreover, if the social utility function is concave it could lead the process to collapse entirely. However, this policy could backfire, because raising the cost of a costly activity may reinforce its signaling power to such an extent that it *incentivizes* more costly variants.

Another approach to undermining a costly norm is to diminish its perceived appropriateness or significance through information campaigns. For example, the demise of footbinding in the early twentieth century was due in part to a campaign that deliberately portrayed it as being old-fashioned and out of step with progressive trends in Chinese society. In terms of the model, this approach can be interpreted as diminishing the social multiplier λ, which can cause the social norm to collapse (as shown by Proposition 7.2)

Yet another type of intervention is to elevate the symbolic value of a less costly substitute. In the case of conspicuous consumption, for example, donating large sums to charitable organizations (art museums, universities, public health initiatives) can serve as a useful substitute for lavish spending on personal goods: it enhances the social status of the donor while channeling the money to useful causes. In other cases, the elevation of an intermediate, less costly action may be effective in undermining support for an existing costly action. As will be discussed in Chapter 8, an intervention of just this sort occurred in the case of FGC practices in Somalia, where religious authorities argued that the less harmful form of FGC (Sunna) is more consistent with Islam than the more traditional, much more harmful version (Pharaonic). The challenge in these and similar cases is to elevate the symbolic value of an intermediate action by enough that it displaces the more costly one temporarily, but not by so much that it becomes entrenched as a new (but still costly) norm.

8

Norms in Transition

Female Genital Circumcision in Somalia

8.1 Background

This chapter illustrates how social interactions models can illuminate the dynamics of norm transition in a contemporary case, namely, the practice of female genital circumcision (FGC). Various forms of FGC are still widely practiced in Africa, the Middle East, and parts of southeast Asia: it is estimated to affect about 200 million women worldwide, and until recently it was almost universal in some countries. As of 2013, for example, the estimated share of cut women was 98% in Somalia, 96% in Guinea, 93% in Djibouti, and 91% in Egypt and 91% in Sierra Leone.[1] This chapter focusses on Somalia, where, over the last half century, there has been a gradual shift away from the most invasive (and physically harmful) form of the practice known as Pharaonic, and toward a less drastic (but still harmful) version known as Sunna, which I shall describe in more detail below.

A key question in the policy debates surrounding FGC is whether the intermediate, less harmful version will serve as a temporary "stepping stone" toward complete abandonment, or whether it is likely to become entrenched as a new norm. In this chapter I show how the framework developed in previous chapters can be brought to bear on this question. I also formulate several criteria for testing whether an intermediate action is likely to serve as a stepping stone as the process unfolds. This issue is of practical importance not only in the case of FGC, but in other situations where policy makers may seek to undermine a harmful norm by introducing less harmful alternatives that are meant to lead toward abandonment, but may have unintended consequences.

The chapter is based on Gulesci, Jindani, La Ferrara, Smerdon, Suleiman, and Young 2025.

[1] Yoder et al. 2013.

The Dynamics of Social Norms. H. Peyton Young, Oxford University Press.
 DOI: 10.1093/oso/9780198959052.003.0008

8.2 Forms of female genital circumcision

FGC is typically carried out on girls aged 8 to 10, although it is sometimes performed at a much earlier age. FGC is deeply rooted in the culture, traditions, and religious beliefs of some communities, and serves as a traditional rite of passage from childhood to adulthood. Ethnographic studies have found that girls who are not cut are often subjected to harassment, mocking, and shunning by others in their cohort.[2] Uncut girls may also have reduced marriage prospects, as some families discourage their sons from marrying a girl who is uncut.[3] (In this respect FGC plays a similar role to footbinding in ancient China, but with the added feature that it has a religious dimension.) Thus there are powerful forces that keep it entrenched as a social norm even though it is known to have serious health risks.

Three principal forms of FGC have been identified by health authorities (WHO 2018). *Clitoridectomy* involves the partial or total removal of the clitoris and/or the prepuce. *Excision* involves the partial or total removal of the clitoris, the labia minora and sometimes the labia majora. *Infibulation* involves clitoridectomy and narrowing of the vaginal orifice by cutting and sealing the labia minora and/or the labia majora. In Somalia, the former two versions are known as Sunna, whereas the latter is Pharaonic.[4] These procedures are typically performed by a cutting professional, who may or may not have medical training. Although infibulation is the most invasive, all of the above-mentioned procedures can have serious health consequences, including increased risk of mortality.[5] Furthermore, since the decision to cut is often taken by the family when the girl is very young, international health organizations have argued that cutting in any of its forms constitutes a human rights violation and is therefore unacceptable.[6]

8.3 Transitioning between forms of FGC in Somalia

The fact that the decision to cut (or not cut) is usually taken between the ages of 8 and 10 enables us to estimate the frequency of each type of cutting in prior years given the age of women that were interviewed in 2020. In this way

[2] Shell-Duncan 2011, Gele et al. 2013.

[3] Mackie 1996. The scope of this "marriage mechanism" has been studied in a variety of settings by Shell-Duncan et al. 2011, Efferson et al. 2015, Bicchieri and Marini 2016, Kudo 2019, Novak 2020, Efferson et al. 2020.

[4] By some accounts, Sunna developed as a substitute for Pharaonic after it was prohibited in some countries by the British colonial authorities (El Dareer 1982, Slack 1988).

[5] For a review of the health risks associated with FGC see Shell-Duncan 2001.

[6] See for example WHO 1982.

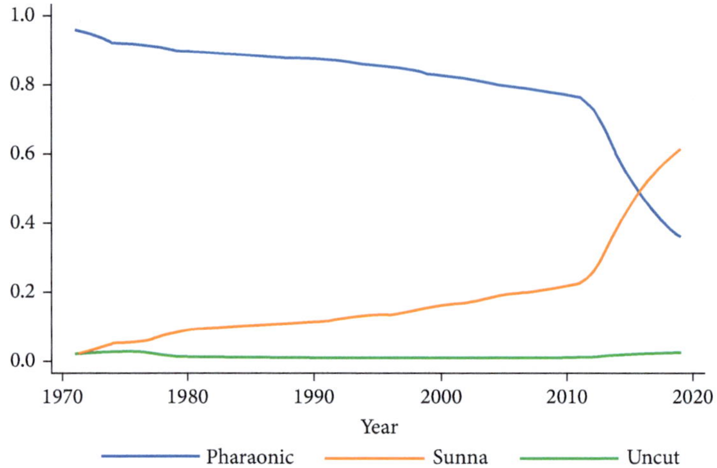

Figure 8.1 Stocks—estimated proportion of women in Somalia who have undergone each type of cut, 1970–2019.

Source: Figure 6 in Gulesci, S., Jindani, S., La Ferrara, E., Smerdon, D., Suleiman, M., Young, H. P. 2025, "A stepping stone approach to norm transitions," *American Economic Review* 115(7): 2237–2266.

we can reconstruct both the flows and stocks of women in each category over a 50-year period (see Figures 8.1 and 8.2).[7] Inspection of these figures shows that, until the late 1970s, almost all girls were cut, and the great majority of cutting was of the Pharaonic type. The next four decades saw a marked increase in the proportion of girls undergoing Sunna, until by the end of the period, Sunna had almost completely displaced Pharaonic among newly cut girls. The proportion of girls who did not undergo either form of cutting remained very low over the entire period, although it appears that there was a small uptick between 2011 and 2019.

8.4 Analysis of the transition dynamics

In analyzing the transition dynamics, we shall be interested in three interrelated questions. First, does a social interactions model with stochastic perturbations provide a reasonably good fit to the data? Second, if we use the estimated model to project the future path of the transition, do we find that

[7] A potential concern with this approach is that it could lead to survivorship bias. To address this issue, we carried out a similar analysis by restricting to women under 40 years old at the time of the survey in 2020. We found that this alternative model exhibits very similar dynamics to the model estimated from the responses of all adult women.

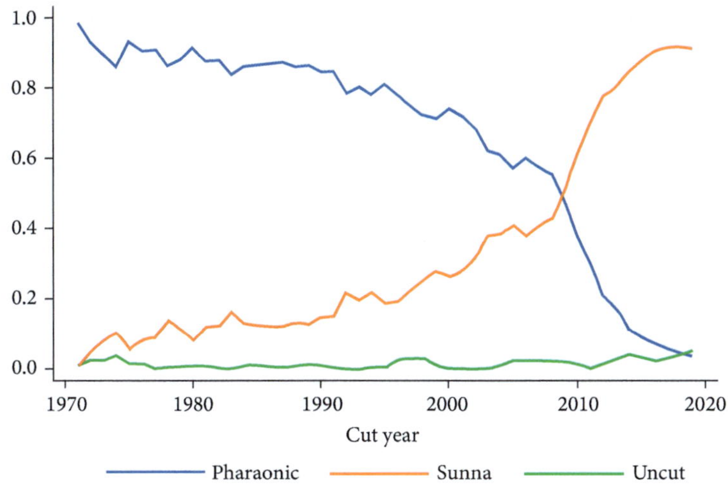

Figure 8.2 Flows—proportion of girls undergoing each type of cut in each year from 1970–2019.

Source: Figure 7 in Gulesci, S., Jindani, S., La Ferrara, E., Smerdon, D., Suleiman, M., Young, H. P. 2025, "A stepping stone approach to norm transitions," *American Economic Review* 115(7): 2237–2266.

Sunna is likely to become entrenched as a new norm, or will it act as a temporary stepping stone on the way to complete abandonment? (The uptick in the proportion of girls not getting cut after 2010 suggests that the latter is a possibility.) Third, if Sunna is absorbing, how large an intervention would be required to tip the dynamics onto a path that leads to eventual abandonment?

To address these questions, we can estimate a social interactions model of the type developed in previous chapters. The *state* at a given point in time is specified by the *stocks* $p = (p_1, p_2, p_3)$, which represent the proportions of adult women with each cutting status at that time: Uncut = 1, Sunna = 2, Pharaonic = 3. The time variable is omitted to keep the notation simple. The *flows* $\sigma(p) = (\sigma_1(p), \sigma_2(p), \sigma_3(p))$ are the proportions of women undergoing each type of cutting (or not cutting) in a given year when the stock variable at the beginning of the year is p. The rate of change in the stocks is therefore proportional to $\dot{p}_i = \sigma_i(p) - p_i$.

The utility of choosing action i consists of its private payoff u_i, minus the social sanction for deviating from others' behavior, plus a random payoff shock:

$$v_i(p) = u_i - \sum_j s_{ij} p_j + \varepsilon_i(p). \tag{1}$$

As we know from Chapter 3, when the utility shocks are extreme-value distributed, the flows can be expressed as follows for some response parameter $\beta > 0$:[8]

$$\sigma_i(p) = \frac{e^{\beta v_i(p)}}{\sum_{j=1,2,3} e^{\beta v_j(p)}}. \tag{2}$$

For every distinct i and j the following linear equation holds, hence we can estimate the parameters of the model using OLS:

$$ln\,((\sigma_i(p)/\sigma_j(p)) = \beta[u_i - u_j - \sum_k (s_{ik} - s_{jk})p_k. \tag{3}$$

The relationship between the coefficients in these regressions and the social interaction coefficients s_{ij} is complicated by the fact that the stock variables satisfy the identity $p_1 + p_2 + p_3 = 1$, hence the coefficient on a given stock variable p_i depends not only on the social interaction coefficients involving action i, but also on the social interaction coefficients involving the other actions.

8.5 Model estimation

It bears emphasizing that this model is highly simplified and does not identify the specific channels that influence the decision to cut. These channels include adherence to tradition and religious practice, a desire to avoid social censure, and a belief that cutting enhances a girl's future marriage prospects; indeed, all of these factors may be present to some degree. I also leave open the question of who is making the decision to cut: ethnographic studies indicate that the girl's parents, particularly the mother, usually make the decision, taking into account health effects, family tradition, and adherence to community norms.[9] The model does not try to disentangle these influences, it simply posits that they create a positive feedback loop between prior decisions to cut and current decisions for girls reaching the age at which cutting is performed. Nevertheless, it turns out that this reduced-form model does a reasonably good job of explaining observed changes in behavior over an extended period of time in the Somalian context.

[8] This model fits subjects' behaviors in experimental settings, as shown in Chapter 4.
[9] Gele et al. 2013.

Table 8.1 shows the OLS regressions of ln (Uncut flow/Sunna flow) against the stocks of Pharaonic (3) and Uncut (1), controlling for district, subclan, and year. Note that all coefficients are highly significant and the R^2-values are above 0.50 except in one case. In Gulesci et al. (2025) we conducted a variety of robustness checks on this estimation. In particular, one might suppose that recent actions weigh more heavily on current choices than actions taken long ago. For example, the decision to be Pharaonic cut in 1980 might not have the same impact on a decision in 2019 as the decision to be Pharaonic cut in 1995. To adjust for this "recency effect," we constructed rolling stocks that only include choices made in the previous k years where $k = 10$ or $k = 20$. We found that the model estimated from these rolling stocks exhibits very similar

Table 8.1 Regressions of $ln(\sigma_1(p)/\sigma_2(p))$ on p_1 *(Uncut)* and p_3 *(Pharaonic)*

	(1)	(2)	(3)	(4)	(5)
Pharaonic stock	3.698 (0.579)*** [0.618]***	5.128 (0.661)*** [0.664]***	5.754 (0.645)*** [0.719]***	4.859 (0.872)*** [0.840]***	5.269 (0.855)*** [0.824]***
Uncut stock	109.721 (18.446)*** [19.436]***	35.132 (7.503)*** [7.246]***	36.578 (13.942)** [14.669]**	72.019 (16.767)*** [16.336]***	72.819 (15.126)*** [14.696]***
Constant	−7.371 (0.643)*** [0.679]***	−6.754 (0.561)*** [0.555]***	−7.227 (0.907)*** [0.995]***	−7.595 (0.849)*** [0.821]***	−8.286 (0.865)*** [0.834]***
Sample	Year	Year–District	Year–District	Year–Clan	Year–Clan
District F.E.	No	No	Yes	No	No
Clan F.E.	No	No	No	No	Yes
Adjusted R^2	0.615	0.562	0.631	0.460	0.536
Observations	38	60	60	58	58

Notes: Observations are years (column 1), year–district (columns 2–3), and year–clan (columns 4–5). Uncut stock is the share of uncut women aged 10 or more in a given year who were uncut and planned to remain uncut. Pharaonic stock is the share of Pharaonic cut women aged 10 or more in a given year. Uncut flow is the share of girls who turned 10 in a given year and were uncut and planned to remain uncut. Sunna flow is the share of girls who turned 10 in a given year and were Sunna cut at some point in their lives. Data for girls turning 10 between 2011 and 2019 were based on stated *intentions* of the family rather than on actual cutting status. Stocks and flows are 3-year moving averages for each year, from 1971 to 2019. They comprise female respondents and all respondents' daughters aged 0 to 18. Standard errors are robust to heteroskedasticity. *p < 0.10, **p < 0.05, ***p < 0.01.

Source: Table 1 in Gulesci, S., Jindani, S., La Ferrara, E., Smerdon, D., Suleiman, M., Young, H.P. 2025. "A stepping stone approach to norm transitions." *American Economic Review* 115 (7): 2237–2266.

dynamics to the model estimated by pooling all prior choices into a single stock variable, as was done in deriving Table 8.1.[10]

One might also be concerned that the model parameters change over time. To examine this possibility, one would need to observe the stocks and flows at more frequent intervals than the annual numbers in the Somalian dataset. However, a partial check on parameter stability was carried out by estimating the model when restricted to more recent stocks and flows (1990–2019). Although the parameters themselves changed to some extent, the overall dynamical path of the model estimated in this way turns out to be very similar to the dynamical path estimated from the full data set.

8.6 Extrapolation test

The estimated coefficients in Table 8.1 can be used to assess whether Sunna is likely to be absorbing by extrapolating the process from the most-recently measured state (the stocks in 2019). This extrapolation is shown in Figure 8.3. Notice that the proportion of Uncut is *nonmonotonic*: first increasing then decreasing. This behavior is not an aberration: there are many specifications of the model parameters that yield similar behavior (see for example Figure 8.4). Assuming that the model coefficients remain fairly stable over time, the extrapolation in Figure 8.3 suggests that the intermediate practice (Sunna) will

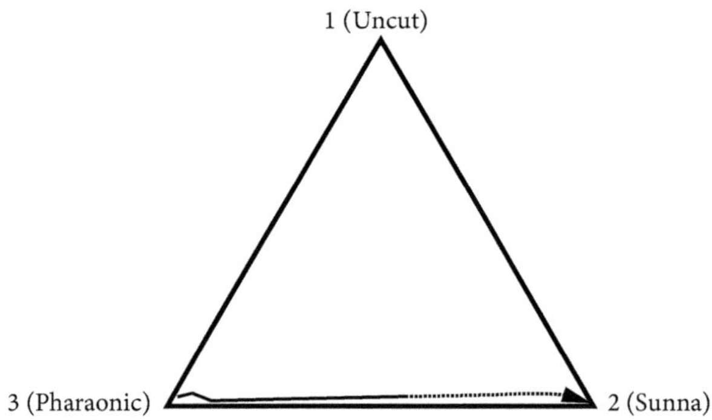

Figure 8.3 Extrapolation of the stocks $p(t)$ based on the flows $\sigma(p(t))$, starting from the stocks in 2019.

Source: Figure 8a in Gulesci, S., Jindani, S., La Ferrara, E., Smerdon, D., Suleiman, M., Young, H. P. 2025, "A stepping stone approach to norm transitions," *American Economic Review* 115(7): 2237–2266.

[10] Gulesci et al. 2025, online, Appendix D.

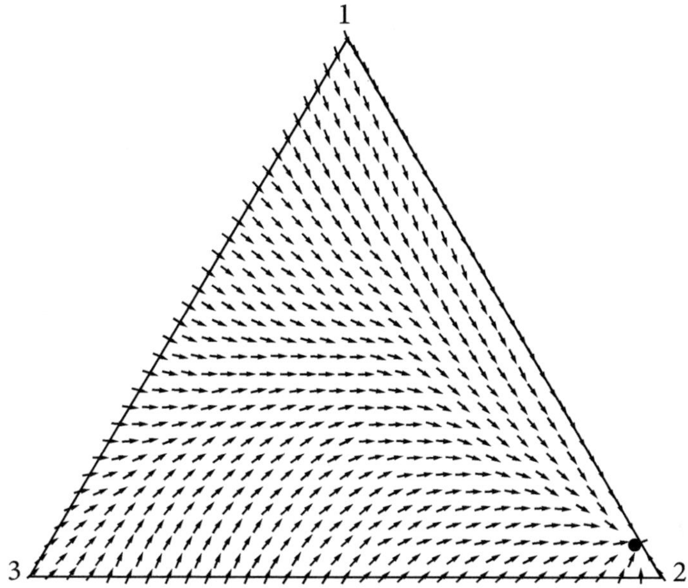

Figure 8.4 Illustration of nonmonotonic dynamics: as action 3 decreases, action 1 first increases, then decreases.
$u_1 = 1,\ u_2 = 0.5,\ u_3 = 0;\ s_{32} = s_{31} = s_{23} = s_{21} = 2;\ s_{13} = s_{12} = 0;\ \beta = 2$

eventually become entrenched as a new norm, and not act as a stepping stone on the way to complete abandonment.

8.7 Reverse triangle inequality test

I now consider a second test as to whether Sunna is likely to be absorbing or to serve as a stepping stone. Recall from Chapter 7 that when there are three actions ordered from least costly (1) to most costly (3), as measured by private costs, a necessary condition for the intermediate action (2) to be a stepping-stone under the best response dynamic is that the social interaction coefficients satisfy the *reverse triangle inequality* $s_{12} + s_{23} < s_{13}$. In the present context, the high-cost action is Pharaonic (3), the intermediate-cost action is Sunna (2), and the least-cost action is Uncut (1). It may be checked that in the regression of $ln(\sigma_1(p)/\sigma_2(p))$ on p_1 and p_3, the coefficient on p_3 (Pharaonic) is precisely $s_{12} + s_{23} - s_{13}$. Thus, a necessary condition for Sunna (2) to be a stepping stone in the best response dynamic is that this coefficient be *negative*. This turns out not to be the case (at a high level of significance) in any of the regressions in

Table 8.1. In other words, this test shows that Sunna is likely to be absorbing under the best response dynamic. Of course, this result does not establish that Sunna will be absorbing in the presence of stochastic perturbations, hence the test is indicative rather than definitive. Taken together, however, the extrapolation and the reverse-triangle test both point toward the conclusion that Sunna is likely to be absorbing, assuming that the model parameters remain fairly stable over time.

8.8 Interventions

I turn next to the question of whether repeated interventions by religious figures and NGOs might have noticeably shifted the dynamics over the period. Interventions by NGOs were aimed mainly at persuading people to abandon cutting altogether, due to its harmful medical effects and violation of girls' human rights.[11] Religious leaders, by contrast, tended to emphasize that the less harmful practice (Sunna) is more in keeping with Islam than Pharaonic. These interventions should have led to an increase in the proportion of girls choosing Uncut and/or the proportion of girls choosing Sunna. On the one hand, Figure 8.1 shows that from 1970 to 2010 there was virtually no increase in the flow into Uncut, which suggests that the interventions were not very effective in getting people to abandon the practice altogether. On the other hand, there was a dramatic acceleration of the flow rate into Sunna during this period. This could have resulted (at least in part) from the interventions, but it could also have arisen purely endogenously through positive feedback effects and no change in the model parameters.

The model provides a handle on the issue of how large an intervention would be required in order to steer the dynamics away from Sunna and onto a path converging to complete, or near-complete, abandonment. In other words, if one could induce a sufficient increase in the stock of Uncut, say through information campaigns about the harmful health effects of cutting, what proportion of Uncut would be needed so that the dynamics take over and finish the job purely through positive feedback effects? Simulations show that if the proportion of Uncut in 2019 were increased to 5% from its actual value of 2.7%

[11] In 1982, the World Health Organization declared it is unethical for female genital cutting to be performed by "any health officials in any setting, including hospitals or other health establishments" (WHO 1982). For a discussion of the debate between advocates of harm reduction and those arguing for complete elimination, see Shell-Duncan 2001.

(and the Sunna proportion were decreased accordingly), the process would transition on its own to mostly Uncut.

8.9 Discussion

The Somalia case study highlights several features of norm transitions that we have seen in other settings. First, although in theory there could be a continuum of possible norms, in practice the available possibilities tend to fall into a few categories that define the salient choices. In the case of FGC these choices are defined by established practices of the cutters. Second, the specific factors influencing individuals' choices are context-dependent, and can only be inferred with any confidence from a combination of in-depth surveys and revealed choice behavior. Several different mechanisms, including family pressure, peer pressure, and concerns about future marriage prospects may all be operating to a greater or lesser degree. Their net effect is to establish a positive feedback loop between individual and group behavior that is the fundamental feature defining the dynamics of norms. A potential application of the framework is to assess the dynamic effects of introducing "harm reduction" strategies in other settings, such as e-cigarettes in lieu of tobacco. Although the aim of such policies may be to create a temporary stepping stone that facilitates ultimate abandonment, the risk is that it may actually impede progress by establishing a new, even more stable, but still harmful norm.

9

Social Change

9.1 Persistence and change

As previous chapters have shown, there are many different mechanisms that can induce norm shifts, including changes in economic incentives, changes in social attitudes, top-down interventions, organized movements, and idiosyncratic variations in people's preferences and beliefs. Here I shall briefly recall some of these mechanisms, and then take a step back to consider situations in which several of these forces are operating simultaneously. The intention is not to present an overarching model of norm dynamics that captures all of these cases, but rather to call attention to the complexities that such a model would need to address. My hope is that this account will stimulate other researchers to extend existing theory to encompass a wider array of real-world examples of norm formation and norm change.

Bottom-up, "grass-roots" change results from the dispersed, uncoordinated, idiosyncratic choices of individuals that accumulate until a point is reached where a social group "tips" into a new way of doing things. These idiosyncratic choices may reflect heterogeneity in individual preferences and beliefs, different sources of information, deliberate experimentation, or random variations in behavior that have no clear explanation. In this way, behaviors that were once considered inappropriate, abnormal, or downright bizarre can become widespread and generally accepted in society at large. Casual forms of dress that are now commonplace in the American business environment would have been considered completely inappropriate in an earlier era. Having a child out of wedlock was once considered scandalous. Divorce used to be rare and had significant reputational implications (for US politicians it was a virtual bar to serving in public office), whereas nowadays it is commonplace and does not carry much if any stigma. Gay marriage was unheard of.

In these and many other cases, norm shifts have been driven largely from the bottom up rather than from the top down. They were also carried along by broader changes in social and economic conditions. Over the course of the twentieth century, for example, legal impediments to divorce were gradually reduced, and divorce became more affordable as economic opportunities

The Dynamics of Social Norms. H. Peyton Young, Oxford University Press.
© H. Peyton Young (2026). DOI: 10.1093/oso/9780198959052.003.0009

opened up for women. As contraception became widely available, and women enjoyed greater ability to support themselves in the labor market, having a child out of wedlock became increasingly a matter of personal choice. The stigma was correspondingly reduced as more and more women elected to make that choice.[1] It should be noted, however, that seemingly exogenous changes, such as reduced legal impediments to divorce and increased availability of child support, may actually have been endogenous responses to shifting views about the acceptability of the behaviors in question. More generally, there is a complex interaction between changes in social attitudes about appropriate behavior, changes in the institutional constraints that are placed on such behavior, and the responses of individuals to these changes.

9.2 Top-down intervention

Given the natural sluggishness with which norms respond to changing conditions, it is not surprising that there have been numerous attempts to try to displace costly or socially harmful norms by deliberate interventions. The most obvious tactics include outright bans, criminal penalties, or the imposition of taxes on the harmful activity. As we saw in Chapter 7, however, such attempts have had decidedly mixed results. For centuries, dueling was banned in many European countries and the penalties for being caught were severe. Nevertheless, the practice continued—indeed, illegality may have added to its allure. Protagonists took precautions to carry out the duel in secluded places and at times when no one else was around. If apprehended they might be taken to court, but frequently the judge would dismiss the case. Enforcement was lax in large part because the practice was common among the professional classes, including politicians and lawyers, so the authorities tended to be sympathetic to the duelists.

In the United States, there have been numerous attempts to outlaw tipping, which used to be viewed as a pernicious norm that was out of place in a democratic society. These local statutes proved to be difficult to enforce, however, and they were repealed within a few years. In the Soviet Union, tipping was specifically forbidden because of its association with former class distinctions; nevertheless, the practice continued unabated. As one guidebook put it: "tipping is forbidden but expected."[2] These and many other examples illustrate the difficulty of instituting norm change by top-down edicts.

[1] Akerlof et al. 1996.
[2] Segrave 2009, p. 68.

9.3 Norm leaders

It seems plausible that norm changes are often instigated by prominent individuals, opinion leaders, influencers, or celebrities, who shift normative expectations by setting an example.[3] This does sometimes happen, but as shown in Chapter 5, it is not as common (or as effective) as might be supposed. Empirical research shows that, in fact, new ideas and ways of doing things frequently spread from the periphery of a social network rather than from central "hubs."[4] The reason is that norm shifts in localized subgroups at the periphery can take hold relatively easily and then spread by contagion from one subgroup to another. In contrast, the ability of centrally placed individuals to effect change is hampered by the fact that, although they can influence many people, they are also influenced *by* many people, and therefore have much to lose by deviating from the prevailing norm.

Nevertheless, there are situations where prominent individuals and celebrities may instigate norm change as a *byproduct* of their behavior. The Prince of Wales appears to have been influential in spreading the fashion of wearing a short jacket to dinner instead of a tailcoat, and he probably had few concerns about what others thought of it. Television celebrities can induce shifts in the behavior of local audiences while being somewhat insulated from their reactions. In Brazil, for example, telenovelas feature glamorous women who have smaller than usual families and may be separated or divorced.[5] These programs are produced by the entertainment firm Globo, whose signal reaches some but not all regions of Brazil. Studies have shown that regions in which Globo is available have significantly higher separation and divorce rates, as well as significantly lower fertility rates, than regions where it is not offered, after controlling for factors that might have determined Globo's strategy to enter a given market.

There are still other cases where norm shifts have been triggered by a confluence of factors that focussed public attention on individuals who were not themselves particularly prominent. In 1955, a seamstress in Montgomery, Alabama named Rosa Parks refused to vacate her seat in the "colored" section of a local bus in order to accommodate a white passenger who needed a seat

[3] Ellickson 1991, 2001, Acemoglu and Jackson 2014.

[4] Centola 2018, 2024.

[5] Chong and La Ferrara 2009 and La Ferrara, Chong, and Duryea 2012. Similarly, Jensen and Oster 2009 show that the entry of cable TV in some Indian states in the early 2000s led to increases in subjective measures of female autonomy, increases in school enrolment, and declines in pregnancy rates.

because the "white" section was already full.[6] Parks was promptly arrested for civil disobedience, and she was subsequently fired from her job in a local department store. She was by no means the first person to defy local segregation ordinances, nor was she particularly prominent. As it happened, however, the National Association for the Advancement of Colored People (NAACP) decided to publicize her case, and she became an internationally known symbol of resistance to racial segregation. Indeed, her status as an ordinary person taking a stand enhanced the symbolic power of her actions.

We can understand this norm shift as emerging from the bottom-up but then given an assist by an organization. The decision by Parks to risk arrest by not giving up her seat was an idiosyncratic choice and she probably had no idea that it would trigger a larger social movement. This type of choice is captured in our framework by random variables that reflect stochastic influences on individuals' behaviors. Similarly, the decision of a particular organization to publicize the case may also be seen as a chance event operating at the group rather than the individual level.[7] The fact that this event and its publicity actually triggered a widespread social movement may also have been due to propitious timing: social attitudes were probably close to a tipping point already, and it didn't take much to push them over into a new norm.

9.4 Local targeting

As previously noted, norm shifts are often easiest to instigate at the local level. It takes fewer interventions to shift expectations and behaviors in a small community of people who interact mainly with each other, than to induce a shift in large, dispersed groups. Once a norm change has taken root in enough local communities, it can then spread or diffuse to the wider population. This *local-targeting* tactic has been employed in many different settings, including the formation of natural foot societies in China and village-level campaigns against FGC in sub-Saharan Africa.

Local targeting only works, however, if the localities in question are relatively insulated from outside influences. A case in point is the attempt to ban tipping in US hotels and restaurants, as discussed in Chapter 2. Some states adopted statutes to outlaw the practice, while in other states individual hotels and restaurants took the initiative by posting signs that tipping would

[6] Brinkley 2005.

[7] Evolutionary models incorporating coordinated actions by subgroups are discussed by Young 1998a, Chapter 9, and Bowles 2004, Chapter 12.

not be tolerated. These efforts were ultimately unsuccessful, in part because there were no natural boundaries to the subgroups needed to sustain the ban: hotels and restaurants frequently cater to out-of-town travelers, who would be unfamiliar with such local rules, and against whom enforcement was next to impossible.

9.5 Diffusion among organizations and polities

In many of the cases treated in the preceding chapters, norm shifts occurred mainly through the agency of individuals. There are other situations, however, in which institutions and organizations are the principal actors. In this case the spread of a new norm may be understood as a bottom-up process *between organizations* in which more and more of them adopt the new way of doing things. This phenomenon may be termed *institutional* norm diffusion. The extension of women's right to vote may be seen in this light, as it occurred in a gradual and piece-meal fashion across different jurisdictions.[8] Starting in the mid-nineteenth century suffragists in the United States organized meetings and rallies to mobilize support for giving women the right to vote. The first successes occurred in the conduct of some local elections, such as school boards. The next step was the adoption of female suffrage for some state-wide offices, and in some cases for presidential elections (but not all elections). These changes occurred on a state-by-state basis because under the Constitution (prior to the adoption of the 19th Amendment), individual states had the power to set their own voting criteria. Once female suffrage had been achieved in a few states, the argument was strengthened for other states to adopt it—an argument that was specifically employed by local suffrage movements.

More generally, researchers have documented a wide variety of cases in which new policies and laws spread from one jurisdiction to another through a process of imitation and learning from the experience of other jurisdictions (often neighboring jurisdictions).[9] This creates a positive feedback loop such that adoption by some jurisdictions increases the probability that others will follow suit. As Walker put it in his influential paper on policy diffusion: "[O]nce a program has been adopted by a large number of states it may become a legitimate state responsibility, something which all states ought to have. When this happens, it becomes extremely difficult for state decision makers

[8] Flexner and Fitzpatrick 1996.
[9] Walker 1969, Gray 1973, Volden 2006, Shipan and Volden 2006, DellaVigna and Kim 2025.

to resist."[10] The resulting dynamics are very similar to those studied in earlier chapters, except that political entities rather than individuals are the principal actors.

9.6 Norms and meta-norms

One of the most powerful instruments for triggering norm change is to shift the perceived meaning or significance of an action, and to place it in a broader context. As previously noted, footbinding in China used to signal high social status and was deemed to enhance a girl's marriage prospects. By the early twentieth century, however, campaigners had succeeded in casting the practice as old-fashioned and out-of-step with the progressive values then being adopted from the West, which hastened its demise. In the case of FGC, a tactic employed by some international organizations has been to argue that *any* form of FGC represents a fundamental violation of girls' human rights to health, given that cutting is usually undertaken without their informed consent.

These cases highlight a general proposition, namely, that the perceived appropriateness of particular forms of behavior depends on normative frames of reference or "meta-norms" that apply more broadly, and which themselves are evolving. Of particular note is the general trend toward the extension of individual rights in different domains, which has been gathering force in many countries over the last several hundred years. Slavery was widespread in 1800 but by the end of the century it had been abolished in Europe and the Americas as one country after another outlawed the practice. Property rights qualifications for voting were gradually loosened and then dropped. Suffrage was extended to women, first in local, then in general elections. Gay rights have become legally recognized. Capital punishment has been banned outright or severely restricted in more and more countries. These changes have tended to occur piecemeal as one political jurisdiction after another joined the general trend. Moreover, the change in norm in one domain (such as the abolition of slavery or extension of suffrage) reinforced analogous changes in other domains.

In previous chapters I have focused on the dynamics of particular norms, but a more complete model would take account of the meta-norms within which particular norms are embedded. These meta-norms exhibit similar dynamics

[10] Walker 1969, p. 800.

and positive feedback effects to the evolution of particular norms: they reinforce and are reinforced by an accumulation of changes in related domains. Modeling the interplay between norms in the small and norms in the large represents a challenge to future research on this topic, and is key to understanding how social change occurs more broadly.

Bibliography

Acemoglu D, Jackson MO. 2014. History, expectations and leadership in the evolution of social norms. *Review of Economic Studies* 82: 423–456.

Acemoglu D, Robinson JA. 2012. *Why Nations Fail: The Origins of Power, Prosperity, and Poverty.* New York: Crown Business.

Akerlof GA. 1980. A theory of social custom, of which unemployment may be one consequence. *Quarterly Journal of Economics* 94: 749–775.

Akerlof GA. 1997. Social distance and social decisions. *Econometrica* 65: 1005–1027.

Akerlof GA, Kranton RE. 2000. Economics and identity. *Quarterly Journal of Economics* 115(3): 715–753.

Akerlof GA, Kranton RE. 2010. *Identity Economics.* Princeton NJ: Princeton University Press.

Akerlof GA, Yellen JL, Katz L. 1996. An analysis of out-of-wedlock childbearing in the United States. *Quarterly Journal of Economics* 111: 277–317.

Ambrose SE. 1989. *Nixon, Vol. 2: The Triumph of a Politician, 1962–1972.* New York: Simon and Schuster.

Andreoni J, Nikiforakis N, Siegenthaler S. 2021. Predicting social tipping and norm change in controlled experiments. *PNAS* 118(16): e2014893118.

Arieli I, Babichenko Y, Peretz R, Young HP. 2020. The speed of innovation diffusion in social networks. *Econometrica* 88: 569–594.

Axelrod R. 1984. *The Evolution of Cooperation.* New York: Basic Books.

Axelrod R. 1986. An evolutionary approach to norms. *American Political Science Review* 80: 1095–1111.

Axtell R, Epstein JM. 1999. Coordination in transient social networks: an agent-based computational model of the timing of retirement. In *Behavioral Dimensions of Retirement Economics*, ed. HJ Aaron. Washington DC: The Brookings Institution.

Banfield EC. 1958. *The Moral Basis of a Backward Society.* Chicago IL: Free Press.

Banks S. 2008. Killing with courtesy: The English duelist, 1785–1845. *Journal of British Studies* 47: 528–558.

Banks S. 2012. *Duels and Duelling.* Oxford: Shire.

Bardhan P. 1984. *Land, Labor, and Rural Poverty: Essays in Development Economics.* New York NY: Columbia University Press.

Bardhan P, Rudra A. 1980. Terms and conditions of sharecropping contracts: an analysis of village survey data in India. *Journal of Development Studies* 16: 287–302.

Barnes CA. 1983. *Journey from Jim Crow: The Desegregation of Southern Transit.* New York NY: Columbia University Press.

Baronchelli A, Loreto V, Steels L. 2008. In-depth analysis of the Naming Game dynamics: the homogeneous mixing case. *International Journal of Modern Physics C* 19: 785.

Battalio R, Samuelson L, Van Huyck J. 2001. Optimization incentives and coordination failure in laboratory Stag Hunt games. *Econometrica* 69: 749–764.

Baumgartner F, De Boef SL, Boydstun AE. 2008. *The Decline of the Death Penalty and the Discovery of Innocence.* Cambridge: Cambridge University Press.

Baumgartner F, Davidson M, Johnson K, Krishnamurthy, A, Wilson C. 2018. *Deadly Justice: A Statistical Portrait of the Death Penalty.* Oxford: Oxford University Press.

Bebchuk L, Fried J. 2004. *Pay without Performance: The Unfulfilled Promise of Executive Compensation*. Cambridge MA: Harvard University Press.

Behrman JR, Kohler H-P, Watkins SC. 2002. Social networks and changes in contraceptive use over time: evidence from a longitudinal study in rural Kenya. *Demography* 39: 713–738.

Belloc M, Bowles S. 2013. The persistence of inferior cultural-institutional conventions. *American Economic Review: Papers and Proceedings* 103: 1–7.

Benaim M, Weibull JW. 2003. Deterministic approximation of stochastic evolution in games. *Econometrica* 71(3): 873–903.

Bernheim D. 1994. A theory of conformity. *Journal of Political Economy* 102: 841–877.

Berry FS, Berry WD. 1990. State lottery adoptions as policy innovations: an event history analysis. *American Political Science Review* 84: 395–415.

Bhandari M, Devereauz PJ, Swiontkowski MF et al. 2003. A randomized trial of opinion leader endorsement in a survey of orthopedic surgeons: effect on primary response rates. *International Journal of Epidemiology* 32: 634–636.

Bicchieri C. 2006. *The Grammar of Society: The Nature and Dynamics of Social Norms*. New York NY: Cambridge University Press.

Bicchieri C. 2017. *Norms in the Wild*. Oxford: Oxford University Press.

Bicchieri C, Jeffrey B, Skyrms B, eds. 1996. *The Dynamics of Norms*. Cambridge: Cambridge University Press.

Bicchieri C, Marini A. 2015. Female genital cutting: Fundamentals, social expectations and change. MPRA Working Paper 72927.

Bicchieri C, Mercier H. 2014. Norms and beliefs: how change occurs. *Iyyun: The Jerusalem Philosophical Quarterly* 63: 60–82.

Bicchieri C, Xiao E. 2008. Do the right thing: but only if others do so. *Journal of Behavioral Decision Making* 22(2): 191–208.

Bilancini E, Boncinelli L, Nax HH. 2021. What noise matters? Experimental evidence for stochastic deviations in social norms. *Journal of Behavioral and Experimental Economics* 90(4): 101626.

Billari F, Philipov D, Testa MR. 2009. Attitudes, norms and perceived behavioural control: explaining fertility intentions in Bulgaria. *European Journal of Population* 25:439–465.

Binmore K. 1994. *Game Theory and the Social Contract, Vol. I: Playing Fair*. Cambridge MA: MIT Press.

Binmore K. 2005. *Natural Justice*. Oxford: Oxford University Press.

Binmore K. 2010. Social norms or social preferences? *Mind and Society* 9: 139–157.

Binmore K, Samuelson L, Young HP. 2003. Equilibrium selection in bargaining models. *Games and Economic Behavior* 45: 296–328.

Bivans J, Gould E, Kandra J. 2024. CEO pay declined in 2023 but it has soared 1085% since 1978 compared with a 24% rise in typical workers' pay. Economic Policy Institute Working Paper, September 19, 2024.

Blume LE. 1993. The statistical mechanics of strategic interaction. *Games and Economic Behavior* 5: 387–424.

Blume LE. 1995. The statistical mechanics of best-response strategy revision. *Games and Economic Behavior* 11: 111–145.

Blume LE. 1997. Population games. In *The Economy as a Complex Evolving System II*, ed. WB Arthur, S Durlauf, and D. Lane. Menlo Park CA: Addison-Wesley.

Blume LE. 2003. How noise matters. *Games and Economic Behavior* 44(2): 251–271.

Blume LE, Brock WA, Durlauf SN, Ioannides YM. 2011. Identification of social interactions. In *Handbook of Social Economics* 1, pp. 853–964. Elsevier.

Blume LE, Durlauf SN. 2001. The interactions-based approach to socioeconomic behavior. In *Social Dynamics*, Ch. 2, ed. SN Durlauf and HP Young. Cambridge: MIT Press and Washington DC: The Brookings Institution Press.

Blume LE, Durlauf SN. 2003. Equilibrium concepts for social interaction models. *International Game Theory Review* 5: 193–209.

Bolton P, Dewatripont M. 2005. *Contract Theory*. Cambridge MA: MIT Press.

Bongaarts J, Watkins SC. 1996. Social interactions and the contemporary fertility transitions. *Population and Development Review* 22: 639–682.

Bossan M-J. 2012. *The Art of the Shoe*. New York: Parkstone International.

Bowles S. 2004. *Microeconomics: Behavior, Institutions, and Evolution*. Princeton NJ: Princeton University Press.

Bowles S, Boyd R, Mathew S, Richerson P. 2012. The punishment that sustains cooperation is often coordinated and costly. *Behavioral and Brain Sciences* 35(1): 20–21.

Bowles S, Choi J-K. 2013. Coevolution of farming and private property during the Early Holocene. *Proceedings of the National Academy of Sciences* 110: 8830–8735.

Bowles S, Choi J-K. 2019. The neolithic agricultural revolution and the origins of private property. *Journal of Political Economy* 127(5): 2186–2228.

Bowles S, Gintis H. 2006. Pro-social emotions. In *The Economy as a Complex Evolving System III: Essays in Honor of Kenneth Arrow*, ed. SN Durlauf and LE Blume. Oxford: Oxford University Press, 337–367.

Bowles S, Gintis H. 2011. *A Cooperative Species: Human Reciprocity and Its Evolution*. Princeton NJ: Princeton University Press.

Bowles S, Hwang H-S, Naidu S. 2010. Evolutionary bargaining with intentional idiosyncratic play. *Economics Letters* 109: 31–33.

Boyd R, Richerson PJ. 1985. *Culture and the Evolutionary Process*. Chicago IL: University of Chicago Press.

Boyd R, Richerson, PJ. 2002. Group beneficial norms can spread rapidly in a structured population. *Journal of Theoretical Biology* 215: 287–296.

Boyd R, Richerson PJ. 2006. *Not by Genes Alone: How Culture Transformed Human Evolution*. Chicago, IL: University of Chicago Press.

Boyd R, Richerson PJ. 2009. Culture and the evolution of human cooperation. *Philosophical Transactions of the Royal Society B: Biological Sciences* 364(1533): 3281–3288.

Boyd R, Richerson PJ. 2022. Large-scale cooperation in small-scale foraging societies. *Evolutionary Anthropology* 31(4): 175–198.

Brock W, Durlauf SN. 2023. Interactions-based models. NBER Working Paper 0258, Cambridge MA.

Brock W, Durlauf SN. 2001. Discrete choice with social interactions. *Review of Economic Studies* 68: 235–260.

Brown LM. 2013. The diffusion of innovations: empirical and experimental evidence. DPhil dissertation, Department of Economics, University of Oxford.

Brown LM, Young HP. 2014. The diffusion of a social innovation: executive stock options from 1936–2005. Working Paper, Department of Economics, University of Oxford.

Burke MA. 2015. The distributional effects of contractual norms: the case of cropshare agreements. Research Department Working Paper 15-7, Federal Reserve Bank of Boston.

Burke MA, Fournier GM, Prasad K. 2007. The diffusion of a medical innovation: is success in the stars? *Southern Economic Journal* 73: 588–603.

Burke MA, Fournier GM, Prasad K. 2010. Geographic variations in a model of physician treatment choice with social interactions. *Journal of Economic Behavior and Organization* 73: 418–432.

Burke MA, Heiland F. 2007. Social dynamics of obesity. *Economic Inquiry* 45: 571–591.

Burke MA, Heiland F, Nadler, CM. 2010. From 'overweight' to 'about right': evidence of a generational shift in body weight norms. *Obesity* 18: 1226–1234.

Burke MA, Young HP. 2011. Social norms. In *Handbook of Social Economics, Vol. 1A*, ed. A Bisin, J Benhabib, and MO Jackson. Amsterdam: Elsevier.

Bursztyn L, Gonzalez AL, Yanagizawa-Drott D. 2020. Misperceived social norms: women working outside the home in Saudi Arabia. *American Economic Review* 110(10): 2997–3029.

Burtless G. 2006. Social norms, rules of thumb, and retirement: evidence for rationality in retirement planning. In *Social Structures, Aging, and Self-Regulation in the Elderly*, ed. KW Schaie and LL Carstensen. New York: Springer.

Carvalho J-P. 2013. Veiling. *Quarterly Journal of Economics* 128: 337–370.

Carvalho J-P, Pradelski BSR. 2022. Identity and underrepresentation: interactions between race and gender. *Journal of Public Economics* 216: 104764, https://doi.org/10.1016/j.jpubeco.2022.104764.

Carvalho J-P, Pradelski BSR. 2024. The representation dynamic and the "normalization" of group differences. *The Journal of Law, Economics, and Organization*, ewae014, https://doi.org/10.1093/jleo/ewae014.

Casari M. 2012. Weak reciprocity alone cannot explain peer punishment. *Behavioral and Brain Sciences* 35(1):21-22

Case A, Katz L. 1991. The company you keep: the effects of family and neighborhood on disadvantaged families. NBER Working Paper 3705, Cambridge MA.

Centola D. 2018. *How Behavior Spreads: The Science of Complex Contagions.* Princeton NJ: Princeton University Press.

Centola D. 2021. *Change: How to Make Big Things Happen.* Little Brown, Spark.

Centola D. 2024. Influencers, backfire effects, and the power of the periphery. In *Personal Networks*, ed. MI Small, BI Perry, B. Pescosolido, and E Smith. Cambridge: Cambridge University Press.

Centola D, Baronchelli A. 2015. The spontaneous emergence of conventions: an experimental study of cultural evolution. *PNAS* 112(7): 1989–1994.

Centola D, Becker J, Brackbill D. 2018. Experimental evidence for tipping points in social convention. *Science* 360(6393): 1116–1119.

Centola D, Macy M. 2007. Complex contagions and the weakness of long ties. *American Journal of Sociology* 113(3): 702–734.

Chandra A, Staiger D. 2007. Productivity spillovers in health care: evidence from the treatment of heart attacks. *Journal of Political Economy* 115(1): 103–140.

Chernow R. 2004. *Alexander Hamilton.* Penguin.

Cheung SNS. 1969. *The Theory of Share Tenancy.* Chicago IL: University of Chicago Press.

Chong A, La Ferrara E. 2009. Television and divorce: evidence from Brazilian "novellas." *Journal of the European Economic Association* 7:458–468.

Cialdini R, Kallgren C, Reno R. 1990. A focus theory of normative conduct: a theoretical refinement and reevaluation of the role of norms in human behavior. *Advances in Experimental Social Psychology* 24: 201–234.

Clark K, Kay S, Sefton M. 2001. When are Nash equilibria self-enforcing? An experimental analysis. *International Journal of Game Theory* 29(4): 495–515.

Clark K, Sefton M. 2001. Repetition and signalling: experimental evidence from games with efficient equilibria. *Economics Letters* 70(3): 357–362.

Cohen WJ. 1957. *Retirement Policies under Social Security.* Berkeley CA: University of California Press.

Coleman JS. 1987. Norms as social capital. In *Economic Imperialism: The Economic Approach Applied outside the Field of Economics*, ed. G Radnitzky and P Bernholz. New York: Paragon House.

Coleman JS. 1990. *Foundations of Social Theory*. Cambridge MA: Harvard University Press.

Coleman JS, Katz E, Menzel H. 1957. The diffusion of an innovation among physicians. *Sociometry* 20: 253–270.

Coleman JS, Katz E, Menzel H. 1966. *Medical Innovation: A Diffusion Study*. Indianapolis IN: Bobbs-Merrill.

Crane J. 1991. The epidemic theory of ghettos and neighborhood effects on dropping out and teenage childbearing. *American Journal of Sociology* 96: 1226–1259.

Delcoure N, Miller NG. 2002. International residential real estate brokerage fees and implications for the U.S. brokerage industry. *International Real Estate Review* 5(1): 12–39.

DellaVigna S, Kim W. 2025. Policy diffusion and polarization across U.S. states. *Review of Economic Studies* 93(3): 1602–1634.

Durlauf SN. 1997. Statistical mechanical approaches to socioeconomic behavior. In *The Economy as a Complex Evolving System, Vol. II*, ed. WB Arthur, SN Durlauf, and D Lane. Menlo Park CA: Addison-Wesley.

Durlauf SN, Young HP, eds. 2001. *Social Dynamics*. Cambridge MA: MIT Press and Washington DC: The Brookings Institution Press.

Edgerton RB. 1992. *Sick Societies: Challenging the Myth of Primitive Harmony*. New York: Free Press.

Efferson C, Vogt S, Elhadi A, Ahmed H, Fehr E. 2015. Female genital cutting is not a social coordination norm. *Science* 349(6255): 1446–1447.

Efferson C, Vogt S, Fehr E. 2020. The promise and the peril of using social influence to reverse harmful traditions. *Nature Human Behaviour* 4(1): 55–68.

El Dareer A. 1982. *Woman, Why Do You Weep*? London: Zed Press.

Eligon J. 2020. A debate over identity and race asks, are African-Americans “Black” or “black”? *The New York Times*, June 26, 2020.

Ellickson RC. 1991. *Order without Law: How Neighbors Settle Disputes*. Cambridge MA: Harvard University Press.

Ellickson RC. 2001. The evolution of social norms: a perspective from the legal academy. In *Social Norms*, ed. M Hechter and K-D Opp, pp. 35–75. New York: Russell Sage.

Ellison G. 1993. Learning, local interaction and coordination. *Econometrica* 61: 1047–1071.

Ellison G. 1997. Learning from personal experience: one rational guy and the justification of myopia. *Games and Economic Behavior* 19: 180–210.

Ellison G. 2000. Basins of attraction, long run stochastic stability and the speed of step-by-step evolution. *Review of Economic Studies* 67: 17–45.

Ellison G, Fudenberg D, Imhof LA. 2016. Fast convergence in evolutionary models: a Lyapunov approach. *Journal of Economic Theory* 161: 1–36.

Elster J. 1989a. Social norms and economic theory. *Journal of Economic Perspectives* 3: 99–117.

Elster J. 1989b. *The Cement of Society*. Cambridge: Cambridge University Press.

Elster J. 1990. Norms of revenge. *Ethics* 100: 862–885.

Engstrom EJ, Pietryka MT, Scott JT. 2022. 75(1): 244–258. Constitutional innovation and imitation in the American States. *Political Research Quarterly* 75.

Ensminger J, Henrich J, eds. 2014. *Experimenting with Social Norms: Fairness and Punishment in Cross-Cultural Perspective*. New York: Russell Sage Foundation.

Entwhisle B, Rindfuss RD, Guilkey A, Chamratrithirong A, Curran SR, Sawangdee Y. 1996. Community and contraceptive choice in rural Thailand: a case study of Nang Rong. *Demography* 33: 1–11.

Fehr E, Fischbacher U. 2004a. Third party punishment and social norms. *Evolution and Human Behavior* 25: 63–87.

Fehr E, Fischbacher U. 2004b. Social norms and human cooperation. *Trends in Cognitive Sciences* 8: 185–190.

Fehr E, Fischbacher U, Gächter S. 2002. Strong reciprocity, human cooperation, and the enforcement of social norms. *Human Nature* 13, 1–25.

Fehr E, Gächter S. 2000. Cooperation and punishment in public goods experiments. *American Economic Review* 90(4): 980–994.

Fehr E, Gächter S. 2002. Altruistic punishment in humans. *Nature* 415: 137–140.

Fehrenbacher JB, Pope RA, Jansen IJ, Alexander JD, Ray BW. 1978. *Soil Productivity in Illinois.* Circular 1156, College of Agriculture, University of Illinois at Urbana-Champaign.

Fisher LM, Yavas A. 2010. A case for percentage commission contracts: the impact of a "race" among agents. *Journal of Real Estate Finance* 40: 1–13.

Fisman R, Miguel E. 2007. Corruption, norms, and legal enforcement: evidence from diplomatic parking tickets. *Journal of Political Economy* 115 (6): 1020–1048.

Flexner E, Fitzpatrick E. 1996. *Century of Struggle: The Woman's Rights Movement in the United States, Enlarged edition.* Cambridge MA: Harvard University Press.

Foster DP, Young HP. 1990. Stochastic evolutionary game dynamics. *Theoretical Population Biology* 38: 219–232.

Foster DP, Young HP. 1991. Cooperation in the short and in the long run. *Games and Economic Behavior* 3: 145–156.

Foster DP, Young HP. 2003. Learning, hypothesis testing, and Nash equilibrium. *Games and Economic Behavior* 45(1): 73–96.

Freidlin M, Wentzell A. 2012. *Random Perturbations of Dynamical Systems.* Berlin: Springer-Verlag.

Fudenberg D, Maskin E. 1986. The folk theorem in repeated games with discounting or with incomplete information. *Econometrica* 54: 533–554.

Furman v Georgia, 408 US 238 (1972).

Gächter S, Renner E, Sefton M. 2008. The long-run benefits of punishment. *Science* 322(5907): 1510.

Gallo E. 2020. Communication networks in markets. *European Economic Review* 129:103545.

Gambetta D. 2009. *Codes of the Underworld: How Criminals Communicate.* Princeton NJ: Princeton University Press.

Gates H. 2015. *Footbinding and Women's Labor in Sichuan.* Abingdon and New York: Routledge.

Gele AA, Bo PB, Sundby J. 2013. Attitudes toward female circumcision among men and women in two districts in Somalia: is it time to rethink our eradication strategy in Somalia? *Obstetrics and Gynecology International* Article ID 312734. Gentlemansgazette.com/tuxedo–black–tie–guide, 2018.

Gigerenzer G, Todd PM, ABC Research Group. 1999. *Simple Heuristics That Make Us Smart.* Oxford: Oxford University Press.

Gintis H. 2010. Social norms as choreographer. *Politics, Philosophy, and Economics* 9: 251–264.

Glaeser E, Sacerdote B, Scheinkman J. 1996. Crime and social interactions. *Quarterly Journal of Economics* 111: 507–548.

Glaeser E, Scheinkman J. 2001. Measuring social interactions. In *Social Dynamics*, ed. SN Durlauf and HP Young. The Brookings Institution and MIT Press.

Goldstein M. 2019. The triumph of the roller bag. *Forbes*, April 16, 2019.

Görges L, Nosenzo D. 2020. Social norms and the labor market. In Zimmerman KF, ed., *Handbook of Labor, Human Resources and Population Economics*, Springer Nature.

Gottlieb S, McCarter R, Vogel R. 1998. Effect of beta-blockade on mortality among high-risk and low-risk patients after myocardial infarction. *New England Journal of Medicine* 339(August 20): 489–497.

Graham BS. 2008. Identifying social interactions through conditional variance restrictions. *Econometrica* 76: 643–660.

Gray V. 1973. Innovation in the States: a diffusion study. *American Political Science Review* 67: 1174–1185.

Gregg v Georgia 428 US 153 (1976).

Guala F. 2012. Reciprocity: weak or strong? What punishment experiments do (and do not) demonstrate. *Behavioral and Brain Sciences* 35(1): 1–15.

Guiso L, Sapienza P, Zingales L. 2009. Long-term persistence. NBER Working Paper 14278, Cambridge MA.

Gulesci S, Jindani S, La Ferrara E, Smerdon D, Suleiman M, Young HP. 2025. A stepping stone approach to norm transitions. *American Economic Review* 115(7): 2237–2266.

Gurerk O, Irlenbusch B, Rockenbach B. 2006. The competitive advantage of sanctioning institutions. *Science* 312(5770): 108–111.

Hammond R, Ornstein J. 2014. A model of social influence on body mass index. *Annals of the New York Academy of Sciences* 1331 (1): 34–42.

Handley C, Mathew S. 2020. Human large-scale cooperation as a product of competition between cultural groups. *Nature Communications* 11: 702.

Harsanyi JC, Selten R. 1988. *A General Theory of Equilibrium Selection in Games*. Cambridge MA: MIT Press.

Hechter M, Opp K-D, eds. 2001. *Social Norms*. New York: Russell Sage Foundation.

Henrich N, Henrich J. 2007. *Why Humans Cooperate: A Cultural and Evolutionary Explanation*. Oxford: Oxford University Press.

Henrich J, Boyd R, Bowles S, Camerer C, Fehr E, Gintis H, eds. 2004. *Foundations of Human Sociality: Economic Experiments and Ethnographic Evidence from Fifteen Small-Scale Societies*. Oxford: Oxford University Press.

Hofbauer J, Sigmund K. 1998. *Evolutionary Games and Population Dynamics*. Cambridge and New York: Cambridge University Press.

Homans GC. 1950. *The Human Group*. New York: Harcourt Brace.

Hood R, Hoyle C. 2015. *The Death Penalty: A Worldwide Perspective*. Oxford: Oxford University Press.

Hopkins E, Kornienko T. 2004. Running to keep in the same place: consumer choice as a game of status. *American Economic Review* 94: 1085–1107.

Hopton R. 2007. *Pistols at Dawn: A History of Duelling*. London: Portrait.

Huck S, Kubler D, Weibull J. 2012. Social norms and economic incentives in firms. *Journal of Economic Behavior and Organization* 83(2): 173–185.

Hume D. 1739. *A Treatise of Human Nature: Being an Attempt to Introduce the Experimental Method of Reasoning into Moral Subjects*. London: John Noon.

Hurkens S. 1995. Learning by forgetful players. *Games and Economic Behavior* 11: 304–329.

Huttegger S, Skyrms B, Tarres P, Wagner E. 2014. Some dynamics of signalling games. *PNAS* 111(suppl 3): 10872–10880.

Hwang S-H, Naidu S, Bowles S. 2024. Social conflict and the evolution of unequal conventions. *Journal of the European Economic Association* 22 (5): 2261–2293.

Illinois Cooperative Extension Service. 1995. Cooperative Extension Service Farm Leasing Survey. Department of Agricultural and Consumer Economics, Cooperative Extension Service, University of Illinois Champaign-Urbana.

Imhof LA, Fudenberg D, Nowak MA 2005. Evolutionary cycles of cooperation and defection. *Proceedings of the National Academy of Sciences of the USA* 102: 10797–10800.

Jencks SF et al. 2000. Quality of medical care delivered to Medicare beneficiaries: a profile at state and national levels. *Journal of the American Medical Association* 284(13): 1670–1676.

Jensen R, Oster E. 2009. The power of TV: cable television and women's status in India. *The Quarterly Journal of Economics* 124(3): 1057–1094.

Jindani S. 2014. A game-theoretic approach to duelling and other social norms. MPhil thesis, Department of Economics, Oxford University.

Jindani S, Young, HP. 2026. The dynamics of costly norms. *The Economic Journal.* https://doi.org/10.1093/ej/ueag091

Kahneman D, Tversky A, Slovic P, eds. 1982. *Judgment under Uncertainty: Heuristics and Biases.* Cambridge: Cambridge University Press.

Kanazawa S, Still MC. 2006. The emergence of marriage norms: an evolutionary psychological perspective. In *Social Norms*, ed. M. Hechter and K-D Opp, pp. 274–304. New York: Russell Sage Foundation.

Kandori M. 1992. Social norms and community enforcement. *Review of Economic Studies* 59: 63–80.

Kandori M, Mailath G, Rob R. 1993. Learning, mutation, and long-run equilibria in games. *Econometrica* 61: 29–56.

Knight F. 1921. *Risk, Uncertainty and Profit.* Cambridge MA: Riverside Press.

Ko D. 2007. *Cinderella's Sisters: A Revisionist History of Footbinding.* Berkeley and Los Angeles CA: University of California Press.

Kohler H-P. 1997. Learning in social networks and contraceptive choice. *Demography* 34: 369–383.

Kohler H-P. 2000. Fertility decline as a coordination problem. *Journal of Development Economics* 63: 231–163.

Kohler H-P, Bereman JR, Watkins SC. 2001. The density of social networks and fertility decisions: evidence from South Nyanza District, Kenya. *Demography* 38: 43–58.

Kreindler GE, Young HP. 2013. Fast convergence in evolutionary equilibrium selection. *Games and Economic Behavior* 80: 39–67.

Kreindler GE, Young HP. 2014. Rapid innovation diffusion in social networks. *Proceedings of the National Academy of Sciences* 111(supplement 3): 10881–10888.

Kritzer HM. 2004. *Risks, Reputations, and Rewards: Contingency Fee Legal Practice in the United States.* Palo Alto CA: Stanford University Press.

Krupka EL, Weber RA. 2013. Identifying social norms using coordination games: why does dictator game sharing vary? *Journal of the European Economic Association* 11(3): 495–524.

Kudo Y. 2019. Political efforts to eliminate female genital cutting: long-term effects on women's health and marriage in West Africa. Working Paper. Institute of Developing Economies (IDE-JETRO), Japan.

Kudo Y. 2023. Eradicating female genital cutting: implications from Burkina Faso. *Oxford Economic Papers* 75 (1): 183–205.

La Ferrara E, Chong A, Duryea S. 2012. Soap operas and fertility: evidence from Brazil. *American Economic Journal: Applied Economics* 4: 1–31.

Leifbroer AC, Billari FC. 2009. Bringing norms back in: a theoretical and empirical discussion of their importance for understanding demographic behavior. *Population, Space, and Place.* DOI: 10.1002/psp.

Lewis D. 1969. *Convention: A Philosophical Study.* Cambridge MA: Harvard University Press.

Liggett T. 2005. *Interacting Particle Systems.* Springer Verlag.

Lim W, Neary PR. 2016. An experimental investigation of stochastic adjustment dynamics. *Games and Economic Behavior* 100: 208–219.

Lindbeck A, Nyberg S, Weibull J. 1999. Social norms and economic incentives in the welfare state. *Quarterly Journal of Economics* 114: 1–35.

Mackie G. 1996. Ending footbinding and infibulation: a convention account. *American Sociological Review* 61: 999–1017.

Mackie G, LeJeune J. 2009. Social dynamics of abandonment of harmful practices: a new look at the theory. UNICEF Innocenti Research Centre IWP–9009–06.

Mäs M, Nax HH. 2016. A behavioral study of "noise" in coordination games. *Journal of Economic Theory* 162: 195–208.

Mailath GJ, Samuelson L. 2006. *Repeated Games and Reputations: Long-Run Relationships.* Oxford: Oxford University Press.

Mallaby S. 2010. *More Money than God.* London: Bloomsbury Publishing.

Manski C. 1993. Identification of endogenous social effects: the reflection problem. *Review of Economic Studies* 60: 531–542.

McFadden D. 1974. Conditional logit analysis of qualitative choice behavior. In *Frontiers in Econometrics*, ed. P Zarembka. New York: Academic Press.

Marshall A. 1890. *Principles of Economics.* London: Macmillan.

Masclet D, Noussair C, Tucker S, Villeval M-C. 2003. Monetary and nonmonetary punishment in the voluntary contributions mechanism. *American Economic Review* 93(1): 366–380.

Mathew S. 2017. How the second-order free rider problem is solved in a small-scale society. *American Economic Review* 107(5): 578–581.

Mathew S, Boyd R. 2014. The cost of cowardice: punitive sentiments towards free riders in Turkana raids. *Evolution and Human Behavior* 35: 58–64.

Mausel PW, Runge ECA, Carmer SG. 1975. Soil productivity indexes for Illinois counties and soil associations. Bulletin 752 College of Agriculture, Agricultural Experiment Station, University of Illinois at Urbana-Champaign.

McFadden D. 1981. Econometric models of discrete choice. In *Structural Analysis of Discrete Data with Econometric Applications*, ed C. Manski and D. McFadden. MIT Press.

Michaeli M, Spiro D. 2017. From peer pressure to biased norms. *American Economic Journal: Microeconomics* 9(1): 152–216.

Mill JS. 1848. *Principles of Political Economy.* London: Longmans Green.

Moffitt RA. 2001. Policy interventions, low-level equilibria, and social interactions. In *Social Dynamics*, Ch. 3, ed. SN Durlauf and HP Young. Cambridge: MIT Press and Washington DC: The Brookings Institution.

Monderer D, Shapley LS. 1996. Potential games. *Games and Economic Behavior* 14: 124–143.

Montgomery MR, Casterline JB. 1996. Social influence, social learning, and new models of fertility. *Population and Development Review* 22: 151–175.

Morris S. 2000. Contagion. *Review of Economic Studies* 67: 57–78.

Munshi K, Myaux J. 2006. Social norms and the fertility transition. *Journal of Development Economics* 80: 1–38.

Myatt DP, Wallace C. 2008. When does one bad apple spoil the barrel? An evolutionary analysis of collective action. *Review of Economic Studies* 75(2): 499–527.

Myers RJ. 1973. Bismarck and the retirement age. Letters, *The Actuary*, April 1973.

Nash J. 1950. The bargaining problem. *Econometrica* 18: 155–162.

National Association of Realtors, 2023. *Code of Ethics, Preamble.*

Newton-Small J. 2008. Obama's flag pin flip-flop? *Time Magazine*, May 14, 2008.

Nicolaides P. 2014. Tax compliance social norms and institutional quality: an evolutionary theory of public good provision. Taxation Papers Working Paper 46–2014. European Commission.

Nikiforakis N, Normann H-T. 2008. A comparative statics analysis of punishment in public-good experiments. *Experimental Economics* 11(3): 358–369.

Novak L. 2020. Persistent norms and tipping points: the case of female genital cutting. *Journal of Economic Behavior and Organization* 177: 433–474.

Nye RA. 1993. *Masculinity and Codes of Male Honor in Modern France.* Oxford: Oxford University Press.

Odell RT, Oschwald WR. 1970. Productivity of Illinois soils. Circular 1016. College of Agriculture, University of Illinois at Urbana-Champaign.

Olson M. 1965. *The Logic of Collective Action.* Cambridge MA: Harvard University Press.

Opp K-D. 1982. The evolutionary emergence of norms. *British Journal of Social Psychology* 21: 139–149.

Osnos E. 2022. The floating world. *The New Yorker*, July 25, 2022.

Ostrom E. 1990. *Governing the Commons: The Evolution of Institutions for Collective Action.* Cambridge: Cambridge University Press.

Paternotte C, Grose J. 2013. Social norms and game theory: harmony or discord? *British Journal for the Philosophy of Science* 64: 551–587.

Phelps CE, Mooney C. 1993. Variations in medical practice use: causes and consequences. In *Competitive Approaches to Health Care Reform*, ed. RJ Arnould, RF Rich, and W White. Washington DC: Urban Institute Press.

Platteau J-P. 2000. *Institutions, Social Norms, and Economic Development.* London and New York: Routledge.

Plato, *The Republic.* Book II.

Posner EA. 2000. *Law and Social Norms.* Cambridge MA: Harvard University Press.

Putnam RD. 1993. *Making Democracy Work—Civic Traditions in Modern Italy.* Princeton NJ: Princeton University Press.

Riello G, Rublack U, eds. 2019. *The Right to Dress: Sumptuary Laws in Global Perspective, c.1200–1800.* Cambridge: Cambridge University Press.

Robertson AF. 1987. *The Dynamics of Productive Relationships: African Share Contracts in Compa:rative Perspective.* Cambridge: Cambridge University Press.

Root J, Sadler E. 2026. A theory of network games Part I: utility representations. https://ssrn.com/abstract=5130393.

Rousseau J-J. 1755. *Discourse on the Origin of Inequality.* Tr. Donald A. Cress. Indianapolis IN: Hackett Publishing (1992).

Saez-Marti M, Weibull JW. 1999. Clever agents in Young's bargaining model. *Journal of Economic Theory* 86: 268–279.

Samuelson L. 1997. *Evolutionary Games and Equilibrium Selection.* Cambridge MA: MIT Press.

Sandholm W. 2010. *Population Games and Evolutionary Dynamics.* Cambridge MA: MIT Press.

Schelling TC. 1960. *The Strategy of Conflict.* Cambridge MA: Harvard University Press.

Schelling TC. 1978. *Micromotives and Macrobehavior.* New York NY: W. W. Norton.

Schwartzbach M. 2022. The meaning of "cruel and unusual punishment." nolo.com.

Segrave K. 2009. *Tipping: An American Social History of Gratuities.* McFarland Press.

Shell-Duncan B. 2001. The medicalization of female circumcision: harm reduction or promotion of a dangerous practice? *Social Science and Medicine* 52: 1013–1028.

Shell-Duncan B, Wander K, Hernlund Y, Moreau A. 2011. Dynamics of change in the practice of female genital cutting in Senegambia: testing predictions of social convention theory. *Social Science & Medicine* 73: 1275–1283.

Shipan CR, Volden C. 2006. Bottom-up federalism: the diffusion of anti-smoking policies from US cities to states. *American Journal of Political Science* 50: 825–843.
Shipan CR, Volden C. 2008. The mechanisms of policy diffusion. *American Journal of Political Science* 52: 840–857.
Skyrms B. 1996. *Evolution of the Social Contract.* Cambridge: Cambridge University Press.
Skyrms B. 2004. *The Stag Hunt and the Evolution of Social Structure.* Cambridge: Cambridge University Press.
Skyrms B. 2010. *Signalling: Evolution, Learning, and Information.* Oxford: Oxford University Press.
Slack A. 1988. Female circumcision: a critical appraisal. *Human Rights Quarterly* 10(4): 437–486.
Smerdon D, Offerman T, Gneezy U. 2020. 'Everybody's doing it': on the persistence of bad social norms. *Experimental Economics* 23: 392–420.
Smith A. 1976 [1776]. *An Inquiry into the Nature and Causes of the Wealth of Nations.* Eds. R.H. Campbell, A.S. Skinner, W.B. Todd. Oxford: The Clarendon Press.
Smith T. 1992. Changing racial labels: from Colored to Negro to Black to African American. *Public Opinion Quarterly* 56: 496–514.
Soumerai SB et al. 1998. Effect of local medical opinion leaders on quality of care for acute myocardial infarction: a randomized controlled trial. *Journal of the American Medical Association* 279(17): 1358–1363.
Stiglitz JE. 1974. Incentives and risk sharing in sharecropping. *Review of Economic Studies* 41: 219–255.
Stone L. 1965. *The Crisis of the Aristocracy, 1558–1641.* Oxford: Oxford University Press.
Sugden R. 1986. *The Economics of Rights, Cooperation and Welfare.* Oxford: Basil Blackwell.
Sunstein CR. 1996. Social norms and social roles. *Columbia Law Review* 96: 903–968.
Tabellini G. 2008. Institutions and culture. *Journal of the European Economic Association* 6: 255–294.
Trop v Dulles 356 US 86, 100–101 (1958).
Twain M. 1880. *A Tramp Abroad.* London: Penguin (1997).
Ullmann-Margalit E. 1977. *The Emergence of Norms.* Oxford: Oxford University Press.
United States v. Real Estate Boards 339 US 485 (1950).
Veblen T. 1899. *The Theory of the Leisure Class: An Economic Study of Institutions.* Macmillan.
Vega-Redondo F. 1996. *Evolution, Games, and Economic Behavior.* New York: Oxford University Press.
Volden C. 2006. States as policy laboratories: emulating success in the childrens' health insurance program. *American Journal of Political Science* 50: 294–312.
Walker JL. 1969. The diffusion of innovations among the American states. *American Political Science Review* 63: 880–899.
Weibull JW. 1997. *Evolutionary Game Theory.* Cambridge MA: MIT Press.
Wennberg J, Gittelsohn A. 1973. Small area variations in health care delivery. *Science* 182: 1102–1108.
Wennberg J, Gittelsohn A. 1982. Variations in medical care among small areas. *Scientific American* 182: 1102–1108.
Wenzel M. 2004. An analysis of norm processes in tax compliance. *Journal of Economic Psychology* 25: 213–228.
Wenzel M. 2005. Motivation or rationalization?: causal relations between ethics, norms, and tax compliance. *Journal of Economic Psychology* 26: 491–508.
WHO. 1982. *Female circumcision: statement of WHO position and activities.* Geneva: World Health Organization.

WHO. 2018. *Care of Women and Girls Living with Female Genital Mutilation: A Clinical Handbook.* World Health Organization.

Yan M, Mathew S, Boyd R. 2023. '"Doing what others do" does not stabilize continuous norms'. *PNAS Nexus* 2 (3), pgad 054.

Yoder PS, Wang S, Johansen E. 2013. Estimates of female genital mutilation/cutting in 27 African countries and Yemen. *Studies in Family Planning* 44(2): 189–204.

Young HP. 1993a. The evolution of conventions. *Econometrica* 61: 57–84.

Young HP. 1993b. An evolutionary model of bargaining. *Journal of Economic Theory* 59: 145–168.

Young HP. 1995. The economics of convention. *Journal of Economic Perspectives* 10: 105–122.

Young HP. 1998a. *Individual Strategy and Social Structure: An Evolutionary Theory of Institutions.* Princeton NJ: Princeton University Press.

Young HP. 1998b. Conventional contracts. *Review of Economic Studies* 65: 773–792.

Young HP. 2009. Innovation diffusion in heterogeneous populations: contagion, social influence, and social learning. *American Economic Review* 99: 1899–1924.

Young HP. 2009. Learning by trial and error. *Games and Economic Behavior* 65: 626–643

Young HP. 2015. The evolution of social norms. *Annual Review of Economics* 7: 359–387.

Young HP. 2024. *Spontaneous Order: How Norms, Institutions, and Innovations Emerge from the Bottom Up.* Oxford UK: Oxford University Press.

Young HP, Burke MA. 2001. Competition and custom in economic contracts: a case study of Illinois agriculture. *American Economic Review* 91: 559–573.

Index

For the benefit of digital users, indexed terms that span two pages (e.g., 52–53) may, on occasion, appear on only one of those pages.

Tables and figures are indicated by an italic *t* and *f*.